THE CABIN

A Tandem Memoir of Life in the Wild

by Louise Ruddle Talbot and David Talbot

Published by Browncroft Publishing Company, LLC
1011 South Tyler Street, Covington, LA 70433
www.browncroftpublishing.com

The Cabin: A Tandem Memoir of Life in the Wild

ISBN: 978-0-9883496-3-6
Library of Congress Control Number: 2013953627

Printed in the United States of America

Book design by Rachel Chotin Lincoln (Browncroft Publishing Company)

THE CABIN
A Tandem Memoir of Life in the Wild

by Louise Ruddle Talbot and David Talbot

Browncroft Publishing Company
Covington, Louisiana

DEDICATION

For my dear mother, who innocently stumbled into the wilderness an unwise and probably spoiled young mother, only to face the test of her life. She not only survived but grew into a capable mountain woman.

ACKNOWLEDGMENTS

As most readers know, a project of this sort is a patchwork of many contributors. Foremost is my mother. Her wonderful words are the strong backbone to which all else is attached.

A special thanks to my editor/daughter-in-law Julie Talbot. It is she, more than anyone, who took all of my memories and my mother's, along with the photos, and somehow created this little book.

Thanks also to Rachel Chotin Lincoln, who took all those old snapshots, patched them up, and made them work in the book. My sister-in-law Earline Talbot saved the old albums from which the photos came, and I very much appreciate her foresight.

My wife Lynn's sister Dawn Brown generously led us through the mysterious book-making process.

My son Eric spent countless hours transferring the old photos from three separate albums to some computer thing so that Julie and I could work over the phone, selecting shots and writing captions. Eric drew the floor plans of what we think the original cabin and the later addition looked like, as well sketching the location maps. I'm grateful to him for all of his contributions.

And finally, my dear older brother Doug helped me time and time again, sorting through common memories with many laughs.

Mom, Shep, and I find a sunny patch to enjoy.

INTRODUCTION

I

There will no doubt be those who say this should have been two separate pieces. Two writers, two time periods, two perspectives. But what I keep coming back to is the fact of it being one place. It's the place that stays; everything else—the people and their trappings, the times and their sensibilities—all change around the place. Even the place itself is in constant flux. Yet it's still there.

So from two accounts, I've made this one piece. The experiences lived through in that singular spot are sometimes remarkably parallel, other times completely divergent; two paths from (or to) the same door.

One side of things is from my mother's point of view. A lively, young, city-bred wife—still a girl, really—with two babes, hauled up into a wilderness her husband barely knew. A home as foreign to her as if she'd been loaded into a spaceship and blasted to another solar system.

The other view is my own, just over a decade later. In her writings and time, I am an infant, a worry, though one swaddled and held close in desperate love. In my account, I am an eleven-year-old explorer, brought to heaven on earth.

One place, two experiences.

II

The earlier chronicle, my mother's, covers the year between the summers of 1933 and 1934. With the Great Depression waging its not-so-civil war on prosperity, Dad had lost his automotive industry job in Oakland, California. His parents and two younger siblings (Pat and Gil) had already left their families (and some social bearing) in the Bay Area, for the little lumber town of Grants Pass, on the banks of the famed Rogue River in Southern Oregon. The naïve solution in my father's twenty-six-year-old mind, like many offspring in the face of trouble, was to turn to his parents—sort of. Actually, Dad's scheme was for his family to occupy a one-room cabin built by his father deep in the mountains of Southern Oregon, living off the land—logging in the summer; mining for gold in the winter. It must have loomed romantic and noble in his mind. My mother was up for it, game—but then, she didn't have much choice, with a thirty-month-old and a newborn in tow. The adventure lasted just over two or just short of three years, depending on which aging relative you talk to.

Mom had at various times aspired to write, and so given the gifts of story-worthy setting and circumstance, she set about pouring her thoughts out on paper. The story of her first year, told in her words, reflecting on her time as a "transplant" as she called it, constitutes approximately half of this account.

Dad (left) and his brother Hayden logging cedar, 1934.

III

My own recollections comprise the yin to my mother's yang.

After our first stint in the woods when I was a baby, we moved back to the Bay Area and lived there for the better part of a decade, my dad working as parts manager at his uncle's fancy Pontiac dealership in San Francisco. My maternal grandmother and step-grandfather lived nearby, and Mom loved having them so handy. But, to be closer to my paternal grandparents, and because my father felt wartime San Francisco had become, in his words, "no place to raise a family," we moved to Grants Pass in 1943. Dad got a job at the Chevy dealership at half his previous salary.

Then, suddenly, Mom was in the hospital. She had suffered a miscarriage, and in the process, it was discovered that she had ovarian cancer. Like so many families, we were without insurance, leaving a massive medical bill after she was treated. Once again, Dad's answer was to move to the mountains, save up, and work the family out of debt. Though Mom now knew all too well what life at the cabin entailed, she also reluctantly conceded the restorative powers of the mountains.

And so, in the summer of 1944, the four of us—Dad, thirty-seven, Mom, thirty-four, my older brother Doug, thirteen, and me, eleven—put the majority of our things in storage, and squeezed ourselves plus a few belongings back into the tiny cabin, beginning what for me was one of the most unforgettable years of my life. Those memories of an indefatigable, twentieth-century Huck Finn, recalled some sixty years later, are offered as the other perspective on this spot in the wilderness—this place we called refuge, or Shangri-la, or exile, or home, depending on the day or even the hour.

After I wrote my own account, I looked back at Mom's telling of her first years at the cabin. It was eye-opening. I realized, perhaps for the first time, how deeply changed she was by her hospitalization, losing the baby, the cancer treatment, and the progression of ailments known and unknown. She never lost her erudite, artistic nature. But by the time of our family's second retreat to the cabin in the mountains, the fun-loving, vibrant woman I remember from my earliest years had been forever tempered. Her love for us was never in question. But only in reading her earlier diary was I reminded of the vivacious personality she had been. Eleven years later, she had become someone different, while the person I was to be struggled to emerge.

The cabin as we found it for our second stay in 1944.

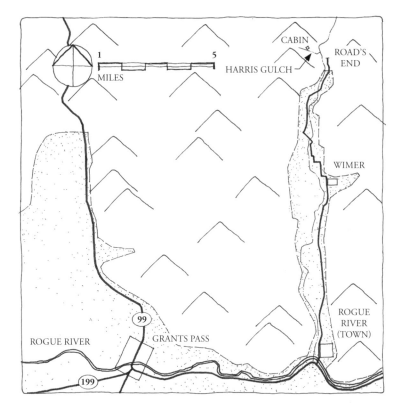

Enlarged Area Map

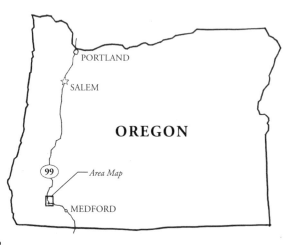

Oregon Map

PROLOGUE
1933-34: Louise

Have you ever been transplanted? I suppose that if a classification were made, I would be called a hothouse variety. Imagine such a breed being torn from its sheltered setting and dropped, defenseless, into the open wilderness. Such is the manner of my uprooting.

From the city's hectic jazz to a wilderness where the rhythm is a stately paced minuet.

July

It is queer to have no pressing engagements. The heaviest commitment is getting three meals a day. I sometimes long for a day and evening pregnant with hilarity, nonsense, futility.

These mountain people never hurry. I have watched and listened to them, sometimes with amusement and then with exasperation. They are so deliberate in their speech and body movements. I do not believe that even an earthquake would animate them.

I know that I am a curiosity, with my lipstick and cigarettes. These mountain women smoke, but only corncob pipes. I can't see why cigarettes should shock them so, but they do.

There are silences and silences. The silence of the early morning. Of hospitals, of death. Of friendship, love, hate. But nowhere have I experienced the devastating silence of these everlasting hills.

I write this as an outlet. I must do something—the

inactivity of this new life is a battle for me. I suppose sometime in the future, my speech and movements, so hurried now, will slow, and become the spaced, drawled-out manner of these strange, distant neighbors.

August

I have just finished the triplicate daily task of doing the dishes. The heat from the stove clings to the room. It will soon be time to light the lamp. I usually forget to fill it until it is time to touch match to wick. Then, I scramble in the confusing gloom for the oil can—again, I have forgotten. I manage to spill three quarters of the can's contents upon the floor, uttering curses as I stoop to mop it up.

I have swept the floor for the sixteenth time today. Either we are very dirty, or very clean.

It is so quiet outside. All the motley crew of birds have let out their last call, and settled for the night. We have a regular nocturnal visitor to the garbage pit. I can hear him now, tin cans clinking. I often wonder what on earth he can find to slake his appetite. He is a beautiful grey, frisky creature. Reminds me of commuting stenogs, shielded by their hundred-dollar squirrel jackets. How many chatterers have gone into each of those coats?

It is so beastly hot; I feel as though I have taken up abode in a Turkish bath. Only wish that I might go around in attire suited to such! This business of building a hot wood fire in the middle of the day is subtle torture.

The lamp is lit. It seems a signal for all of the mountain's winged insects to dash madly for the cabin. Up my sleeves, down my blouse, always coming to rest upon the exact place I am reading!

The madronas are losing their leaves. Contrary leaves! Shedding their clothes in the midst of summer. Crooked trees, twisted with limbs the color of flesh. They remind me of sin.

I glance around this cabin. At the exposed studs. The guns, the rows of saws, and my pictures slung in between. One exotic print should grace a pale-tinted, stuccoed wall. It has no place in these earthy surroundings, but it is a reminder.

It is really dark now. I go outside to search for the Little Dipper, for there in the distance where it hangs is home. To the south, friends, and Mother. The stars are bright. The lamp is a dim yellow shadow on the ground.

September

The heat still hangs on. This evening the coolness of a wind-washed forest is a relief. The swaying trees sound like a distant river, unceasing. I lay upon my back, watching their impressive heights. The small pines are like dancers. The older ones stand unbending and disapproving.

The dogwood trees have put out seedpods. How lovely a few would look in my old blue pitcher, but I have not the courage to strip them. Better to leave them without raw gashes, as Nature meant them to be.

The creek in the canyon below has vanished to a mere trickling driblet. The heat has sapped the creek like it has sapped everything else. Grass, trees, earth all cry, "Parched, parched, water, water."

I am tired tonight. Just physically, not mentally. How I would enjoy a roomful of people arguing about everything, and nothing. But there is just the sound of the high wind, and the call of an owl, and silence . . . silence . . . silence: a crushing weight!

Another Sunday, but unless I knew that the calendar denoted such, I would say it was Monday or any other day. In the cities stores are closed, people are going to evening church services or theatres, or dining in brightly lit restaurants.

I shall start a fire and make coffee and fix myself something to eat. The kindling must be chopped, and the water brought up from the creek.

Another day tomorrow. I close the door, light the lamp, and break the silence with the clatter of the stove.

October

All of the leaves are changing. The dogwood and the oak are red. The maple and poplar are yellow. Seedpods are on every tiny plant. The squirrels are busy robbing cones for their winter stores. They squeak and scold, running merrily up and down the steep trunks. Autumn is approaching so slowly that no one realizes her occupation until we awake one morning to find grey skies and a landscape of frost.

Everywhere, people and animals are getting ready for the siege. Hillsides echo the sound of many axes. Once in awhile, one is surprised to hear the put-put of a gasoline drag or buzz saw. Fuel for the onslaught. From now until the first snow, the prevailing greeting along the road and at the store will be, "Got your wood in yet?"

When I first came here, I could not get over the gargantuan woodsheds alongside tiny cabins. Now I realize the need for those yawning depths filled to the doors with neatly split lengths of wood.

Before I can think, the snow will be falling, the rains will torrent down. The winds will occupy skies that today are a glaring blue.

November

I miss the streetlights, the traffic noise. The stillness is louder than any city's clamor. I never noticed the stars to be so bright before. Here they shine, true celestial lights. The trees, trees, trees, stand so solemnly, like elders of the church. I can almost see their piously crossed hands flopping their coattails.

It is odd to think that no one will ever come ringing the doorbell. No merry clatter, or sound of gears in the driveway. But then, I have neither a doorbell, nor a driveway. Just two weed-grown tracks that swerve drunkenly down the slope, missing trees and gulches. The door stands wide until the chill of night or distant yipping of coyotes close it. I hitch my chair a little closer to the lamp.

Sometimes I feel that I can't stand the quietness—the monotonous, incessant stillness! It is silly, but I hesitate to break it with even a cough. The crackle of brush tightens nerves; how foolish I feel when a small bird hops innocently out!

It is only when the teakettle stops its hum that I jump up to find the stove's last embers glowing up at me mockingly.

December

I have been crossing the days off the calendar. An airplane passes over once a week. I think about those soaring aloft, and wonder whither they are bound. I can almost time the plane's arrival to the minute. Sometimes it heads east, and I have to strain to find it in the distance.

Christmas is almost here. All of our ingenuity is brought to play, for there is no money to be spent at the general store on "boughten" things. Knives and axe make bows and beautiful toys; boxes come into being. I make candy, and ovensful of cookies and cakes. I never before bothered to make these things. I think of my grandmother in her pioneer country, and for the first time appreciate her life. Gram was always humored in her odd idea that hands were made before stores and machinery. Her "I remember when" always fell on deaf ears. What I would give to see her!

We are gathering small cones to gild, and popping corn to string. I have even cut out bits of colored paper to make chains, something I have not done since grammar school days.

While I make divinity and fudge and pray that it will set, my eyes watch the clock, timing the bread, for I usually forget to take it out in time. My books invite me, alas! But for the first time in months, I do not stop to take one or two of them down for a few minutes of browsing. Time is not heavy upon my hands. I am too busy thinking of what I shall serve for Christmas dinner to ponder on Lucretius. Hurray!

Just a few thousand years ago a man died . . . I think of the world today . . . no doubt the Prince of Peace would have been branded for a Red, and treated accordingly! He stirred a revolution, and soon we will celebrate his birth. Strange world, but I do hope that all of us aren't too busy to think back and remember the real reason for Christmas.

I wonder how long it will be before the city will see me again? Right now I do not care much, but I know I want to go back. When I get there, will I be satisfied to stay away from these hills?

January

For almost two weeks the land has been receiving its white coat of snow. I find myself mesmerized watching the flakes as they appear, high against the slate-colored sky, following their descent. Something, usually the fire in need of wood, jerks my attention from the paned window.

Icicles hang stiff from the eaves; leaves show their dripping sword points. The trees are like half-closed umbrellas, so heavy are their burdens of snow.

I have become resigned to the imprisoning whiteness. Inside, I chafe at my confinement, but find it does little good to fight Nature. She is master of everything here.

All creatures are revealed in this white blanket. Deer tracks are deep holes, with trailing hoof points. Squirrel imprints are tiny and shallow. Birds' marks are funny little crissy-cross scratches, like a child's first attempt with a pencil.

The silence now is of such soft deepness. There is something of Death in it; the quietness of its approach, its cold finality.

Each night I go out into the darkness, and lift my face to the cool touch of the flakes. There is to me a touch of ceremony, a prayer in those few seconds before I go in and bank the fires for the night.

February

The snow has almost vanished. Patches are like chunks of broken frosting on a very large chocolate cake. It is fun now to step on the patches left on the trail. Just a few weeks ago, my weary feet rejoiced at finding a bare spot of ground in which to rest before taking off into the piled drifts again.

There is a positive sense of glee in feeling a stretch of good, brown terra firma underfoot. Little patches of green are showing beneath protecting logs, and around tree trunks. The birds seem glad to see the snow melting. They are quite bold in their late winter desperation, approaching the door for food scraps.

There is a fragrance not quite definable in the air. Damp sprouting earth and new growth. The creek is almost torrential, roaring day and night. I grow quite morbid watching its flow; it is going somewhere, but I seem to always be standing still.

I can almost tell the time of the year by the rows of wood left in the shed. It was stacked full in October; now it has a gaping hole. Every time I bring in an armful of sticks and see them stacked beside the stove is a satisfaction. How odd it is to become so intimate with these things.

Never before in my life have I felt the completeness that envelops me now. I sit reading, snug beside the lamp, listening to the roar of the fire with its companion wood box filled to the brim, while the storm rants, subsides, rants again outside. I wonder why I should desire more.

March

The days pass like shadows across my face, scarcely perceptible. Once in a while, a day stands out clearly from the rest. A day of violence. A day of sunshine that only fades into a black night of steady rain.

Surely, spring shall never come! And then, an unfolding fiddleneck fern gives evidence of the coming.

The tree toads are singing again. I like their friendly croaking voices. Reminiscent of old seamen, hoarse with the brine of many oceans upon their throats. In the shaded dusk they begin quite unnoticeably, one at a time, with their solos.

Along the trail, I find the funny tracks of a 'coon, meandering along my private right-of-way. So far, we have never met. The only contestant to my rights to date has been a skunk, and I said, "You first, my dear Alphonse," and prayed his name was Alphonse. One does not offend a skunk! There is a chipmunk that lives in a dead fir tree alongside the trail, and he dares to tell me I trespass. How he scolds! I stop, and soon he sticks his inquisitive nose out—quick as a flash he is gone again. I daresay, I must make an amusing picture!

If I go tramping in the hills I never see a wild creature. But if I sit quietly and unmoving upon a dead log, my eyes soon see movement amongst the greenness of trees and brush. They seem unaware of me, and I can watch to my heart's content. I think of their kin, whom I've seen in zoos. I wonder which is better off, the wild animals, free but vulnerable to predators, or their cooped-up kin, protected and fed? In spite of the danger, these wild things seem far happier.

April

I quite suddenly seem to have had a veil removed from my eyes. I am vividly aware, conscious of the world.

Conscious of the Earth as a pulsing, breathing thing. I want to lay myself as close as possible to its rhythms.

I walked down the trail, and hearing a stirring in the brush, paused to listen and look. Silence, and then in a bit—out stalked a pheasant. Soon I distinguished the female. There, the wonder of spring was enacted before my eyes. That male! Strutting, preening, and the little female seemingly oblivious to it all. But I knew better.

A giant pine, grey, staunch, and grizzled as a wizard caught my eye. How often I passed this tree. Blind mortal. See there? On the outstretched twigs are new green tips! The birds are all back; the robin, the cedar waxwing, the swallow. They all show themselves, decorating the bud-dipped trees.

The creek is swollen by a thousand little rivulets. Cow tracks cut the sloppy trail; they are heading into the hills, higher places. They know the sprouting grass, and where it grows. Higher and higher they go every day.

May

Was there ever anything as red as a robin's breast in a slanting silver rain? I stopped to watch them, caught up high in a drift of wind. I felt exalted.

Underfoot, the grass is springy and soft. No rug could be more luxurious. Only those who have never experienced new sprouting grass after months of snow and rain-drenched, sodden-leafed ground can appreciate this carpet.

No artist, I am sure, could depict to my satisfaction the richness of rolling pasture in its green spring dress, with trim of robin's red. I have seen chiffon, but never any like the sheer fabric of grey rain against the pasture hills today.

June

Summer is upon the soft noon hours.

The lizards and snakes are showing themselves mid-day, sunning in the patches of light. How somnolent they are, still as though dead. Against the dirt they are indistinguishable, and I am startled when their scuttle betrays their bodies close to my feet. Are they startled too? How shivery they are, yet they swerve. The bees are out, too. Insects have hatched and died in hatching. Birds are building nests. All things, even the trees, are starting new life in their individual manner of birthing.

The miracle of the seed! I too, have taken part in this bringing of new life, with my garden. How grand it is to push little seeds into the brown earth. Then, alone within the warmth of the soil, they begin their little journeys, simultaneously down-rooting like babies and pushing up, breaking the crust of the soil.

These hills have changed me as fire changes iron. I seem to have gone through a process of finishing. Somehow the petty things of life have died; ignoble deaths with no one to mourn their passing. Time and the hills, healers of my body and my soul. I came, rebellious and afraid, and now I am content. Each day, borrowing a little of the serene oblivion of the hills. My soul must indeed resemble these hills, the jagged scarred peaks, and the smoothed, rounded roll of the furrowed lowlands.

Chapter 1
Summer, 1933: Louise

David was gurgling to himself, in the bassinet we had strung up under the canvas top of the roadster. I hoped that his milk, which I had tried to keep warm in a Thermos bottle, would agree with him. His two-and-a-half-year-old brother Dougie's little legs kept beating a tattoo against the back of the seat. Despite his leg movements, Dougie was asleep with his head against my arm; I hardly dared move. I turned to look at my husband Doug, the dashlight a reflection against his face. Conscious of my scrutiny, he turned to smile reassuringly. For one moment, his hand left the wheel and clasped mine. I needed that clasp. Four human beings in one old roadster. Four human beings bound for a new world.

With the hum of the motor in my ears, I found my mind jumping from one thing to another. Had I left anything I would need? I peered up at the bassinet, listening for the baby's breathing. Such a tiny, sick baby! Just six weeks old. I remembered the doctor's warning that he wouldn't guarantee the baby's life if I took him away from medical care. For a moment my mind frantically reviewed the baby book, remembering all the catastrophes that could happen. I didn't know a thing! Dougie sighed, and changed his position. Reassured, I shifted him into a more comfortable position. I had never really had the sole care of Dougie, thanks to my mother's loving assistance. Looking ahead at the curving road, my heart was heavy.

I pictured my mother's home, Doug standing in the living room, saying the unfathomable: out of a job! Then, Mom's face as she stood in the driveway at home, seeing us off. Such consternation,

In California just before moving to Oregon in 1933. Mom with an unhappy Doug, Dad with an oblivious me.

My mother's stepfather and mother, Joe and Mabel Hanson. They lived not far from us in Oakland, California, and my mother was very close to them. Mom's birth dad was Elmer Ruddle, who died in an industrial accident when she was little.

as she dramatically yelped, "You can't start off today! It's Friday the thirteenth!" I giggled and told Doug our journey was DOOMED! Poor Mom, she hadn't cried at our leave-taking. Her amazement at our decision to move to Oregon was as real as her worry. How would the four of us live on $240 a year—$20 a month? We put up a bold front, but when we were alone together, we too had been afraid.

David began to whimper, and I asked just how much further did we have to go? Doug looked at the river and the speedometer—only about ten more miles to his folks' place, where we would breakfast. Then they would lead us up to our new home.

The river gleamed in the dawn. I couldn't help but be thrilled at the silver sound. I again questioned Doug about the cabin. My mind had repeatedly rejected his descriptions in favor of the picture I preferred: a log lodge, of the type I had seen frequently in the movies, replete with a huge fireplace, stag heads, etc. He turned, looked sternly into my eyes, and again warned me not to expect anything of the sort. But I knew that men as a general rule knew little of these things, and I would have to see for myself. After all, it was on 640 acres of virgin timber. Never having been out of the city in my life, I had no real comprehension of what that meant. It was a lot of land, though. Surely there must be a suitable home to preside over that kind of spread.

Suddenly, Doug said, "See that white house there? That's the folks' place." I nodded, lowered my head between the bassinet and Dougie's head, and squinted at the small sign of civilization drawing closer. "Yes!" I exclaimed, in the joy of finally arriving someplace, anyplace. I struck as dramatic a pose as possible in the cramped space. "Here we are, the modern pioneers, in our covered wagon!" Doug chuckled and said, "I don't know about pioneering, but this is a pretty fancy conveyance alongside the ones that came across the plains and mountains into Oregon." I retorted my wish that we had a covered wagon, one of those canvas-covered trucks like the CCC drove, so that

I could have brought my desk, the crib, all of my books . . .

Doug interrupted, *"Yes, you'd have brought the whole house along, no doubt, but as it is, this car is so overloaded that the rear springs are almost on the ground. Be satisfied that you argued me into bringing what you did, including those books."* My precious books had culminated in a family row. I proclaimed I would not be going to Oregon or any other faraway place without my books, and I meant it! Doug tried to chisel the box's contents down, but I refused to leave out any of the chosen few. Over the steep Siskiyous there had been several times when I thought the weight of the rear end would land us all in a terrible wreck at the bottom of a deep canyon.

We pulled up in front of Doug's parents' house. I shook Dougie awake and told him he could announce our arrival to his grandparents. Scrambling out, he raced into the house.

Soon thereafter, we were at the breakfast table, David dry and fed. Oh, how good the food tasted! Now that we were here, I didn't want to go any farther.

All too soon, we were in the cars and on our way, Doug's parents escorting us on the last leg of our journey. I gazed unbelievingly at this little town, as we drove down its one main street, past a hotel—if such a broke-down, weary building could be called such. But yes! There was a sign proclaiming it the Waldorf Hotel! A cousin of the salad and New York's Waldorf Astoria, perhaps. I stared at the chickens roosting on the sagging veranda and at the munching cow tied to a paling fence minus half its picket. A grey-bearded old man teetered on a kitchen chair and returned my gaze blankly.

As if that hotel wasn't enough to catch my attention, the store where we stopped to pick up a few things certainly was. Here was a huge barn of a place, with the window displaying a pair of shoes circa 1915 or thereabouts, alongside stacks of soaps and canned goods with their paper wrappers, wrinkled with age and covered with fly specks, *all reposing upon lengths of ancient crepe paper. Inside, I found the great-granddaddy of all stoves. It was vast, and around it in a circle sat five men, as alike as peas in a pod to the gentleman at the Waldorf. Long grey beards and overalls, all with the same blank, uninterested look upon their faces. They bothered me. I wanted to look, and yet every time I turned my head I found five pairs of solemn eyes upon me.*

The store seemed to sell everything from straight pins to tractors. The storekeeper, a rather stout man, moved about, getting our things together as though he had all the time in the world and then some. I found myself mentally shoving him to go faster, but it did no good. Finally, we had everything, and turned to leave. The proprietor cleared his throat and spat at the stove, hitting it dead center. I jumped as he aimed, but I needn't have worried. He drawled, "You folks aiming to settle here?" I looked at Doug; he looked at me. Neither of us seemed capable of speaking. We nodded our heads, dummy fashion, and dashed out the door. There we stood, trying to keep straight faces. It didn't work

En route to the cabin, we stopped at my Talbot grandparents' beautiful home on the banks of the Rogue River, just outside of Grants Pass. Left to right: Dad, my grandmother, Doug (in Mom's arms), Dad's brother Gil, Mom, Dad's brother Hayden, Dad's sister Pat. At six weeks old, I'm probably sleeping in the house.

and we finally dissolved in laughter. We were in a foreign land, sure enough!

Out of town was by way of a standard oiled road, and it seemed to stretch for miles through the valley. The towering hills in the distance were awe-inspiring to me. Doug pointed north and said, "Behind that peak is our cabin." I stared and stared until the whole rolling scene became a blur. I gulped and held David tighter, pulling Dougie up against me, gaining strength from their nearness. The hills looked so grim! I realized I was frightened. Doug pointed out the passing farms. They looked poor to me, but Doug seemed enthusiastic, so I agreed that they were nice spreads, as he called them. A mailman passed us in a sedan and I realized I had no idea how we were to get our mail.

"This is rural free delivery up here," he replied, "and the mailman comes as far as the Hardins' place on the country road. We live about six miles from there. I asked Mr. Hardin if we could have our mail delivered at his box, and—"

"Six miles?!" I was stunned. Why, I had never walked six miles in all of my life! Doug smiled, and remarked to the passing scenery that pioneer women thought nothing of walking fifteen to twenty miles for food, let alone mail. At that remark I began to get angry. I wasn't a pioneer. I had tried to be a good sport, but this was 1933, not 1833.

Several miles passed in silence. Then Doug looked sideways at me, smiled, and jeopardizing the safety of us all, took both of his hands from the wheel and hugged me to him. I smiled back, sighed, and began to ask questions again. Were our nearest neighbors the Hardins? Doug said no, there were two old miners just a few miles from the cabin. Men—what good were they? Doug said they seemed like very nice gentlemen. I looked down at the baby, and considered how badly I might need a woman's advice.

Suddenly, the road got very bumpy, and I was hard put to hang on to the baby while not banging my own head. We were winding around a mountain now. The rear lights of Doug's parents' car flashed in and out of sight ahead of us. Those grim peaks were directly overhead, plunging us into half darkness. Overhanging trees and brush scraped the car. The curves grew more eccentric. I heard running water, and there it was: a lovely stream, rushing past on our left. Pleasant Creek, I would soon learn. Then the road dipped, and the stream was directly in front of us. But where was the bridge? Before I had a chance to say a word, we were in the water with a churning of wheels and clashing of gears! I was amazed! Out on the other side, I exhaled and realized I'd been holding my breath. I looked at Doug, and he howled, saying my face had been a study! I didn't think it amusing at all. Up a steep pitch, and then the car was bucking like a ship in choppy seas. But as suddenly as it started, it stopped. Doug called it a corduroy road, and explained how the road bottom was laid with small trees like matches, creating a base that wouldn't wash out when the rains came. What a country!

Now up another steep pitch, and into the tall timbers' shade. I tried to see their tops, but couldn't. Silence and shade. I felt like I had entered a cathedral; the sound of the motor was loud, so loud in my ears. I opened my mouth, but shut it again. God was here, I was sure, and I was a mere human, struck speechless and frightened.

Another curve—and suddenly there was a small building. Another abandoned miner's shack. But the car ahead was slowing, as were we. I looked at Doug, who smiled back, encouragingly. I let my eyes travel over a structure that had no relation whatsoever to the cabin of my imagination. This? This was to be my home for the foreseeable future? There were no masterfully honed logs, no wide porches full of rocking chairs. This was a shed, and not a large one at that, built of planks and battens, with a tar-paper roof. I sat there in the car clutching the children to me. I wanted to run—run back the way we had come, to my mother, paved streets, the sound of traffic.

No one paid the slightest attention to me as I sat motionless in the car. Everyone was busy unloading the cars, unlocking the cabin, bringing in the supplies. I sensed they understood how I felt, and thought it better to leave me alone until my mind readjusted to what lay before me.

Finally Doug roused me, saying I needed to come see the cabin.

Cabin? I had no desire to see what was inside this misnamed excuse for a home. But out I went with the children. Dougie was entranced, staring up at the tall trees. I swallowed hard, looked at my husband, and, close to tears, turned toward the building. Dougie ran ahead, then stopped, turned, and asked, "Mommy, where are the sidewalks?" With that to break the tension, everyone laughed.

There were three steps up to the covered porch, which led to the front door and the interior. Could any space be as unattractive? It was a single small room, perhaps twelve feet by twelve feet. Straight ahead was the back door. The bare beams and exposed studding made me cringe, the furnishings were of the simplest fashion: a small sheet-iron stove for cooking, slightly rusted; a Franklin stove for heating; a table with one leg propped up with a block of wood; two chairs; and a daybed. Along one side were plank shelves; the opposite wall held rows and rows of saws. Saws shining and sharp, with ragged teeth that gleamed in the light. There were three windows, so small that even with the door open there wasn't enough light to see plainly. This one tiny room was our home. I held my breath, braced myself, then slowly turned to everyone and pronounced, "Not bad, is it?"

Despite my words, I must have looked like I had lost my last friend, for Doug promptly suggested that his parents take their leave so we could settle in to our new home. I smiled gamely and waved as they pulled away.

I stood at the door looking out into the darkness, listening to the night noises. We had the bassinet for David and a small bed for Dougie, and they had both fallen fast asleep in no time.

The sound of a twig cracking startled me, and up the hill I saw two red eyes reflected in the light from the cabin. I was overwhelmed by an unreasoning fear of this place, with its silence that shouted louder than any noise.

Our water would come from the creek, fifty feet down a

steep trail and back up via a bucket. Doug approached with the next morning's supply and stood alongside me.

"Smell that air, will you?" he asked.

"I can't smell anything, all I can do is hear the nothingness and see the staring eyes," I replied.

He looked off into the night, saying that there wasn't anything to be afraid of, and that I must school myself to not imagine things that were not there.

"Not there?! What are those eyes I just saw, and what is that over by the creek stealing through the brush? Nothing, I suppose?! If I could only see them!"

Doug picked up the water buckets, and went in the door. "We'd better get to bed. Tomorrow will be a hard day for all of us. At least we have a roof over our heads, and the sure prospect of food, which is more than most people have these days," he philosophized, but his voice sounded odd. For just a moment I wondered if he felt as I did, frightened and doubtful, but being a man, and head of his family, he had to appear nonchalant in the face of almost anything.

I wasn't in a Pollyanna mood, but the occasion seemed to warrant such a display, so I followed him into the cabin, saying, "I know we're lucky, but only time will tell how this will work out. I wish we had something to drink with, and something to drink! Seems like our safe arrival calls for some sort of a celebration!"

Doug said that he for one was going to celebrate by going to bed, and I followed. As I lay there on the hard mattress with David in his bassinet beside me, watching Doug load the gun and put it alongside the bed, lock the doors, and turn down the wick of the lamp, myriad recollections of the day flashed through my mind in a kind of kaleidoscope effect. I still hardly knew what the cabin looked like, though goodness knows I had stared at it long enough! Beneath the tall fir, cedar, and pine, it looked like a doghouse to me! Under the towering timber, I knew that no matter which direction I looked, there would be nothing but trees—just trees and more trees. In my mind, I reviewed the long road, the miles we had come from the folks' place.

Miles and miles; here we were in a strange land among strange people, as surely as if we had sailed for Europe or Asia.

Doug turned and whispered, "Gee, it is quiet, isn't it?"

The children's regular breathing filled the room, along with the squeak of the bedsprings and the occasional eerie hoot of an owl. I thought of all that lay ahead of me, and wondered how I could possibly learn to build a fire, do laundry without a machine, and cook. Well, I could try. I turned and asked Doug why he had brought a loaded gun to bed with us, only to be answered by no answer. I alone was awake in the darkness. I thought of Mother, and wondered if she was thinking of me, too. I remembered my grandmother kneading bread in her sunny kitchen, and knew I would soon be doing the same without the sunniness or the kitchen. David moved in his sleep; the bassinet rocked on the pine-slab bench. I put out my hand, and found him uncovered. I slipped out and covered him, and then went to stand by the window. The moon had come up, and the shadows were deep. Shadows that moved and seemed to take shape, only to dissolve before my gazing eyes. Suddenly, something moved outside the door. I held my breath, listening. There it was again. I could hear a sort of a snuffling sound, and a scraping.

Terrorized, I found myself shaking Doug and screeching that there was a tiger or a bear, or something outside the door, and for him to get up, and take the gun, and shoot it!

Staggering with sleep, Doug finally roused himself enough to get the flashlight, in the meantime saying that whatever was or had been there, had surely been frightened away by all my yelling, and for gosh sakes to calm down!

My teeth were chattering with nerves as I watched him creep to the door with gun in one hand, flashlight in the other. He opened it a crack and shone the light outside. My heart thudded, and I held my breath. With a flinging gesture, Doug threw the door wide open, laughing so hard that I could hardly understand what he was saying.

"There's your tiger and bear!"

And there, in the light's beam, stood a huge porcupine, more terrified than me, if that was possible.

We returned to bed, Doug ribbing me until he fell asleep again. I did feel silly, and determined then and there to try to control this wild imagination of mine, or else I would surely have the whole family in a continuous state of turmoil.

Chapter 2
Summer, 1944: Dave

D_ad_ had called a meeting with my brother Doug and me. I had just finished fifth grade, Doug would be going into ninth. We were living in Grants Pass, a pre-adolescent boy's paradise: a small lumber town surrounded by so much wilderness—and wildness—that we never ran out of places to explore. In fact, the house we lived in sat so close to the hills that we could escape civilization in a matter of minutes, which we did often.

Dad got right to the point, as usual.

"What would you boys think about the family moving up to the cabin for a year or so while I try to get us out of debt?" My mother's recent miscarriage and cancer treatment had left piles of medical bills that we knew weighed heavily on our parents. But upon hearing the apparent consequence, we had to blink twice. Were all adult problems solved so miraculously?

Dad would make the thirty-mile commute to his job in Grants Pass twice daily. When school started, I would attend elementary school in the tiny community of Wimer, Doug would go to high school in Rogue River. Mom would hold down the fort in the cabin.

Our words couldn't jump from our mouths fast enough. "Yes, yes, yes! When do we leave?!"

After moving to Grants Pass in 1943, we'd often spent

summer weekends or longer periods at a tiny family cabin nearly thirty miles away in the mountains. From Grants Pass, you took what is now the old highway on the south side of the Rogue River to the little town of the same name. After crossing the bridge over the river and driving through town, you would then head due north. The road rose to a small crest where the beautiful Evans Valley lay before you. Pavement ended in Wimer, which was no more than a few gas pumps, a small store, and an equally small grade school. In the far distance, tucked between large peaks, were three small mountains. Our cabin was on the farthest of the smaller mountains, about halfway up.

As you drove, the farms and ranches became farther and farther apart, until there were no more. Nobody lived beyond us.

At around twenty-five miles, before you got to our place, the county route turned into to a narrow, two-lane dirt road. From that, you turned onto an even more primitive track. Our closest neighbors, the Johnsons, lived just before the turnoff. After dropping down and fording Pleasant Creek, a steep climb then delivered us to a small open meadow, where a cabin once occupied by two old Alaska Gold Rush bachelors my mother called "the Charlies" (they were both named Charlie) was still standing in 1944. From there on up to the cabin, perhaps a quarter of a mile, the pitch was not so severe.

Cabin time was about as good as it got for my brother and me: gallivanting around the forest in all manner of gameplay, long walks stalking the elusive wild strawberry, and the precious small jars of jam that would be the pay-off for our foraging.

The coolness of the shaded hillside and higher elevation seemed to help Mom's asthma—another affliction that had dragged down her spirited nature over the past few years.

Once the decision was made to move to the cabin, we started hauling our lives up there in boxes and carloads. We went to work on numerous projects—summer was waning, and much needed doing before the winter rains and snow.

When we moved back to the cabin for our second stay, in the summer of 1944, the road was so bad, only a tractor could navigate what was left of the crude route. Grandad drives while my grandmother (in the hat), mother, and I ride.

The road was a priority. The little ruts leading up to the cabin slowly dropped down to beautiful little Pleasant Creek where a car could ford at low water in the summer. That year, the rains had almost obliterated the two-rut path, with erosion cutting huge troughs in many places. Fixing the road was time-consuming, pick-and-shovel work that introduced me to blisters. But it would facilitate transport of all winter food supplies, plus materials for a planned bedroom addition. In the summer, Mom and Dad slept in a bed in the corner of the cabin's one room, and Doug and I slept on the porch. But colder weather would require different accommodations for us.

Once the road was made passable, work on the new bedroom quickly commenced. Added to the north side of the existing cabin, it almost doubled the structure's square footage. Doug and I were impressed with how Dad planned and put it all together. We helped, too, and it was fun watching it slowly rise. Then, one day, there it was! Doug and I each had a metal army cot, while Mom and Dad had a bed in the other corner of the room.

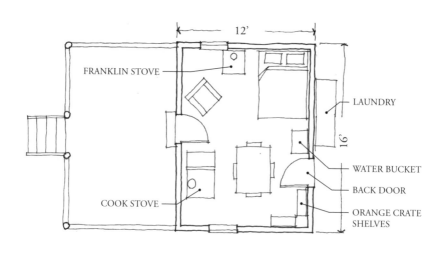

FRANKLIN STOVE

LAUNDRY

12'

16'

COOK STOVE

WATER BUCKET

BACK DOOR

ORANGE CRATE
SHELVES

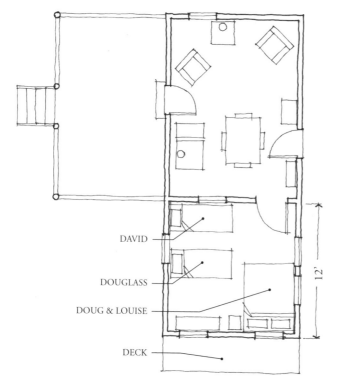

DAVID

DOUGLASS

DOUG & LOUISE

DECK

12'

(Above) During our first stay in 1933, we all squeezed into the cabin's one small room, no more than a couple hundred square feet. (Below) For our second stay, Dad built an addition that provided a bedroom for all of us.

An addition to the cabin gave us twice the space—which still wasn't much.

I think there were three windows and like the original room, the ceiling was open to the rafters. If you like the sound of rain on the roof, you would have loved it—I certainly did.

As we labored on these projects, we knew we were working against the coming fall rains, when Pleasant Creek would rise and end access to the cabin by car. We made as many motorized runs as possible, knowing everything would soon have to be packed in on our backs.

Another project was putting by the winter wood. Getting the fuel to the fire was no mean feat. The plentiful madronas made great firewood but they were real axe-breakers due to their density, and chain saws hadn't yet been invented. Pine was pitchy. So, the choice was fir—but as Dad explained, not just any fir. It had to be close to and preferably uphill from the cabin, for transport efficiency.

A short distance up the old road behind the cabin, we found one that made the grade: about three feet in diameter; straight and tall. Felling a tree is both art and science; the trick was to make it fall onto the road, which was somewhat level and free of brush and other obstacles.

The first step was the undercut, a major means of "aiming" the tree toward its final resting place. Doug and I took either ends of a two-man crosscut saw. Approximately two feet from the ground, we made a foot-deep slice into the tree. Then, starting maybe eight inches below the saw cut, we chopped up toward the new cut, using a sharp, double-headed axe.

Next we went to the other side of the tree and sawed perhaps ten inches above the opposite undercut. As the cut ate its way into the tree, the trunk's stability wavered. In a deft feller's hands, the undercut causes the tree to fall in that direction. But even for the most skilled timberman, this remains one of the most dangerous jobs in logging. Trees fall where they want.

"Let the saw do the work, boys, just gently pull it back and forth and let the sharp teeth do their job," Dad patiently encouraged us.

As the two cuts drew closer, he had us stop sawing and hike up the hill to gauge where the tree would fall. Finally, as the cuts were almost touching, he stopped us and placed a wedge in the saw-made cut on the backside. He then began slowly driving the wedge deeper and deeper into the tree, reminding us of the pre-determined safe place we would run to when the towering giant decided to go.

Suddenly, a deep, guttural sound filled the air. From the center of the trunk, a voice seemed to whine and groan—low and tentative at first, then gaining volume. Our wide eyes instinctively rose to the top of the tree as it started to lean—slow, then farther and faster, crashing through branches of nearby trees and picking up momentum by the second.

Dad dropped his sledgehammer, simultaneously yelling "Timber!" at the top of his lungs. We all sprinted to the safe place. The deafening roar of ripping wood and the thunderous "WHOOMP" as it hit the ground were terrifying. A massive cloud of dirt, branches, and brush flew into the air.

And then, just as suddenly, there was an eerie silence.

We looked at what only a moment before had been a majestic, centuries-old living monument. By luck or my father's expertise, it had fallen mostly in the road.

We didn't mourn the tree's demise, that sentiment wouldn't become popular for another several decades. But there was an unspoken understanding of just how quickly we had demolished a project Mother Nature had been working on for hundreds of years.

Getting the tree cut up and ready for the stove would take us another month of hard work. The trunk was probably one hundred and fifty feet long. Branches had to be cut—some as thick as eight inches across. Then came the tedious job of sawing through the fallen tree. As you might expect, such a boring and physically demanding project is fruitful ground for disagreement between two brothers—each sure the other is not pushing or pulling hard enough. Doug and I got on either side and began to work the saw. We soon learned that Dad's advice of "slow and easy, let the saw do the work" was best. It seemed like it took forever to make one clean-through cut—Doug remembers it taking about thirty minutes, my mind has it closer to thirty hours.

"Sh, sh, sh," the saw slowly ate into the tree. One thing in

Finding, cutting, and hauling wood was a big part of our lives.

40

our favor was the increasing narrowness of the trunk the farther up we got. Finally the tree had been transformed into a pile of fair-sized rounds. Now they just had to get to the cabin. We stood each round up on its edge, like a wheel, and with each of us on either side, rolled it down the road. Some rounds decided they didn't need our help and galloped down on their own, usually soaring off into the forest. Getting them back onto the road was a job unto itself.

Once arrived at the cabin, the rounds were laid flat. Our job was to reduce each round into pieces small enough to fit in the kitchen and Franklin stoves. Using a wedge and a maul, the round would be split into halves, quarters, eighths. The eighths were then axe-chopped to sizes that would fit the stoves.

Finally, in a contest to see who could carry the biggest armloads, we bore our prized fuel to the back of the cabin and stacked it in the crawl space underneath. Soon Doug and I would be trading weeks, making sure the wood box was always full for heating, cooking, and boiling water. But for now, we had a new bedroom, the road was passable, the larder was stocked, and the wood that would see us through the coming winter was packed snugly under our feet.

###

For Mom, Doug, and me, daily routines were dominated by the complications of life "off the grid" as we would refer to it today.

There was no plumbing—indoors or out. The toilet was a traditional two-holer outhouse a short distance from the cabin, where last year's "Monkey Ward" catalog had been placed for a visitor's reading pleasure.

Sometime during that first stay in the '30s, Dad devised a scheme to eliminate the tedious hike down to the creek for water. He went upstream to a point where a diversion ditch could be built

Our super-deluxe, two-holer outhouse.

Dad's brother Hayden at our improvised flume. This was our water source for everything: drinking, cooking, and cleaning.

to carry water downhill to a spot very close to the cabin. There he built a makeshift flume from which we could fill buckets to carry to the house. Keeping the ditch and flume open and free of debris became one of our many chores. When returning with a bucket of water, we would sometimes slowly start it swinging, back and forth, higher and higher, picking up momentum until it would swing completely over our heads, going round and round without spilling. Ah, the wonders of centrifugal force. Once to the back door of the cabin, the bucket would be placed on a stand, above which hung a traditional ladle, which was the source of many a long, gulping slurp of icy mountain water.

There was no electricity. Kerosene lamps were used at night. To light them, you first had to fill the small bowl at the base of the lamp with kerosene. Then the clear, tall chimney was removed and the small knob was turned, raising the wick, which extended down into the kerosene. You lit the wick with a match. Next came the tricky part. The sustained light you were hoping for came from a flimsy and delicate object called a mantle. As you turned up the wick flame, the mantle would slowly begin to glow, brighter and brighter until it reached the level you desired. If you turned it up too fast, you risked burning it beyond repair, which in turn required an expensive new mantle. Once the lamp was correctly ignited, the chimney was replaced and a shade placed on top. If you were close enough, there was enough illumination to read or write.

The little cooking stove was adequate for heating most of the time, but sometimes we cranked up the Franklin for extra heat. Old Ben had dreamed up a unique design whereby the front section could be removed, offering a full view of the burning wood within—the next best thing to a fireplace.

I don't remember much about laundry days because I tried to stay as far away from that production as possible, lest I be recruited to help. It must have been a terrible chore for Mom. First, water had to be heated on the stove—lots of it. The hot water went into the washtub (outside the back door as I recall) with the washboard, against which the dirty clothes were rubbed and scrubbed. She also needed hot water for rinsing. I can remember coming home from school and finding the entire main room adorned with wet clothes, hanging from every possible surface and protrusion, on wooden clothes racks, and even from the rafters. In the cold winter months it almost got foggy in there from the wet and steamy clothes.

When all the chores were done, we would gather around the kitchen table. There was no radio reception, so Mom taught Doug and me how to play three-handed bridge as we waited for the sound of the car announcing Dad's arrival. I think my love of geography began there, also. We often played "Cities" at the dinner table. I started with Astoria, the person on my left had to name a city starting with the last letter of my city, in this case another A. They might say Ashland and the next Dallas, and then Salem, and so on until someone couldn't think of the next city.

Our distance from civilization notwithstanding, World War II was very much a part of our lives for most of that year. The war in Europe and the Pacific had turned in our favor, but rationing of basic necessities was still required. Gasoline, tires, sugar, even shoes were in limited supply and required special stamps to purchase. Dad had been deferred from military duty because he was in his thirties and had two small children. However, his two younger brothers were both serving—Hayden with the Navy in the South Pacific and Gilbert flying P-51s in England. His younger sister Pat's husband Bob was fighting the Germans with the Army in Italy.

###

Summer always brought the forest alive, and in the warm months of 1944, there was lots of activity in our neck of the woods. Just down from our cabin, thirty yards or so away, stood an old chicken coop left over from our visit in the '30s. Dad decided that we should have some chickens and rabbits. I was to take care of the chickens and Doug the rabbits.

Doug (left) and me, with a family friend home on leave from World War II. Our rifles, from the previous Christmas, were the bane of any small animal that moved.

We soon repaired the indoor roosting area and chicken-wire-fenced space where they spent their time scratching around in the dirt during the day. We secured six or seven hens and one crusty old rooster. Dad was told that the rooster liked whiskey, so for weekend family entertainment, Dad would pour a little fire water in an old lid and we would watch the rooster drink it, then stagger around, sometimes falling but always picking himself back up. They say necessity is the mother of invention, but I would argue boredom plays a big part, too.

Dad and Doug built three rabbit hutches. These were little cages on four legs with chicken-wire floors. Those rabbits! The stories about how fast they can reproduce are true. There was a lot of rabbit on the menu that year.

Of the many wild critters that tormented our lives, skunks and their relatives, civet cats (or spotted skunks), were high on the enemy list. No matter how hard we tried, we couldn't keep them out of the henhouse.

Doug and a smelly neighbor who liked our chickens.

Most of the summer, Doug and I slept out on the porch where it was always cooler. It was great to sleep out there, snug in our beds, talking and listening to the night sounds and the muffled voices of Mom and Dad talking inside. One night on the porch, Doug and I were awakened by a commotion in the direction of the sleeping chickens. We quickly grabbed a flashlight and Dad's .22 rifle and crept silently toward the henhouse. Slowly opening the door, we flipped on the flashlight. If you haven't raised chickens, they sleep sitting side by side on broomstick-like wooden poles, off the floor and to the back of the hen house.

There, sitting brazenly right amongst the sleeping chickens, was a skunk, holding a chicken by the neck. Both the chicken and the skunk turned to look at the light with what can only be described as surprising nonchalance.

The trick in killing a skunk is to somehow shoot it in the head and pray that it dies before releasing that unmistakable, potent odor. It never worked. After these encounters, I would have to hold my nose for a week when entering the henhouse.

Mom and Dad had tried to grow a vegetable garden on their visit a decade earlier, and for some reason hadn't learned their lesson the first time. An optimistic attempt to produce at least some of our own vegetables was undertaken again. Clearing even a small patch of forest and getting the soil ready for planting was—and always will be—high on my list of onerous tasks. Brush and trees above ground; root systems and rocks below. Worse still, any success was perceived by the four-legged locals as a generous all-you-can-eat buffet.

One weekend afternoon that summer, Abe Johnson, our closest neighbor, came to talk with Dad about building a bridge across Pleasant Creek the next spring. While exchanging pleasantries, Abe reached into his jacket and brought out a small canning jar containing what appeared to be water, but was far from it. "White lightening," as they called it, was pure alcohol. Small glasses and water were soon procured and set on the table. A small amount of moonshine was added to about a third of a glass of water. I remember something of a simple toast; down it went. Within maybe a second, Mom and Dad were both choking,

Digging up brush roots for our "garden" gave us a blistering respect for the pioneers.

gasping for air, and wiping tears from their eyes. Before drinking, Abe reached into his mouth and removed the baseball from his cheek—well, that's what I thought it might be, but the mess he hauled out was, it was explained later to me, chewing tobacco. We also learned later that having a small still back in the mountains for producing white lightening was common practice.

It was an informative afternoon.

Chapter 3
Summer, 1933: Louise

My eyes opened to the sun pouring in the small window over our heads. David was uncovered again, and Dougie was sitting up in his bed, looking entirely accustomed to awakening in such a place as this every morning. Doug's place beside me was empty, but I heard the sound of an axe and the cry of several birds. For the first time I noticed the lovely scent of the timber. Looking around, I began to rearrange everything in my mind. I thought of curtains, and the making of shelves, and the problem of how one made pancakes here, and how was I ever going to bathe the baby in someplace so drafty? Cheered, I arose, dressed, and faced the new day in our new home with confidence and much curiosity.

In the daylight, and not suffering from shock as I had the day before upon arrival, I began to get the lay of the land. The cabin sat in a very pretty but precarious setting, on the edge of a steep creek. The structure was braced in the back with huge pieces of timber to keep it from sliding down the bank during the winter rains. In front, the ground also sloped sharply away. In fact, it seemed that wherever I looked, the land was either going sharply up, or steeply down!

There were few level spots, and those were rocky, with roots jutting out. Poor little Dougie was having a difficult time of it. He had come in with various bumps, bruises, and scratches already. I could see that the medicinal supply would have to be replenished at once. But children do seem to accustom themselves quickly to almost anything, and Dougie was soon galloping and puffing up and down, following his daddy wherever he went, and often going where Daddy wasn't. The *day before, I had heard the far-off sounds of his crying, and went to investigate. He had tried to climb over a fallen log, gotten his fat little legs twisted in the branches and was unable to get up. Doug and I had talked as seriously as anyone can to a child that age about the dangers of getting out of sight of the cabin, about rattlesnakes and poisonous bugs. I couldn't be six places at once, and Doug had his jobs to do. Between us, we worried our heads off about the toddler. We just had to cross our fingers and hope. I thanked my lucky stars that David was a baby; I didn't know what I would have done if I'd had two active children to keep an eye on. As it was, I was continually dashing out the door to listen, and then to call, "Dougie, where are you? Answer Mommy . . . " If he didn't answer immediately I broke out in cold perspiration, immediately envisioning his little self wandering lost in the timber, or meeting up with a snake and bending over to look—!*

Things were still helter-skelter. I tried to find a place for everything, but there was no place to put anything. Nails were pounded into the walls to hang our clothes upon, and a packing box was turned into a dressing table. An old dress became the skirt. I was proud of my handiwork. David alone of all of us had a place for his clothes. Incongruously, there sat his white, silk-lined wicker wardrobe. I moved

The cabin from across the ravine. How many houses come with a sledding hill just outside the front door?

50

the few pieces of furniture from one spot to another, trying to find the place where they would show to best advantage. I had wrapped some of my better china in my mother's velvet piano cover; this became a drape for the high window, complete with drawstring, so that I might be able to shade the baby's bed at midday. I had a vision of my mother's shocked face as I cut and sewed the soft length of velvet!

We stopped at noon to prepare another meal, which was to be my job alone for the first time. Doug brought in small bits of wood and larger broken branches, and explained the rudiments of making a fire. I felt rather superior as he explained, for hadn't I been a Camp Fire Girl? And as everyone knows, one thing a Camp Fire Girl learns is how to light a fire. How smug I was as I went about my business. First the paper, then the twigs and some larger branches—then the match! How simple! I guess the wood didn't know I was a Camp Fire Girl because it refused to do more than send up a bit of blaze, then promptly die out. Three times I repeated the procedure, growing more impatient and angry with each attempt. Then—a brainstorm! Kerosene! Just a little of that on the darned fire, and it would surely burn! No sooner thought of, than done. Complacent and confident, I put a match to the stove.

The room exploded in a terrific roar and blast of air. I staggered backward as all four stove lids rose majestically into the air and then fell back. David screamed with fright. Stunned, I was touching my singed eyebrows, eyelashes, and hair, when Doug came pouncing into the cabin demanding to know what the devil I'd been up to?! As casually as I could, I said, "Oh nothing, I just couldn't get that darned fire going, so I put some kerosene on it, and it sort of blew up." The fire was blazing alright, and I looked at Doug. He was literally pulling his hair and growling in a level, gritty tone, "Haven't you any sense at all? Do you realize you could have set the whole cabin on fire, and maybe even started a forest fire?"

"Well, you can just make your own dang fires—" My defensiveness was cut off by the sound of a truck coming up the road. It was Doug's folks, and we went out to meet them.

Dad climbed out of the cab, and said something about getting a block of wood behind the rear wheels to keep it from rolling, but stopped in mid-sentence as he saw me. "What on earth happened to you?"

To save my soul, I couldn't think of a word to say. How I hated to have proved myself incompetent the very first day!

Doug looked grim for a moment, then broke into a smile. "She is a pretty sight, isn't she? Oh, she tried to build a fire, and when it wouldn't burn, she had the bright idea of pouring half the kerosene can on it!"

I'll just pass over the lecture that I had to listen to for the next hour. Suffice it to say that from that time on I was the most devoted student of fire building you'll ever meet! But, to this day, I can't build a decent fire without a bit of pine pitch, or oodles of dry kindling! I guess it's just a natural talent, like gardening, or having a light hand with biscuit dough.

Dad suggested that we have lunch before beginning the arduous task of unloading the supplies. After glancing at the heavily loaded truck, I agreed.

I don't quite know what I expected regarding the "supplies," but I certainly didn't imagine having a complete grocery store moved into our already-crowded cabin! Cases of milk, and canned vegetables, fruit, and meats. Sacks of flour, sugar, potatoes. Boxes of dried fruit, milk, and eggs—yes, dried eggs! Coffee in ten-pound tins, syrup in five-gallon cans. Sides of bacon, and whole hams. It was all piled up and up, in a steadily growing stack in the middle of the floor, until I could hardly get around it to pick up the baby. Where were we going to put all this stuff? And how could we ever eat it all? When Doug came in with a twenty-five pound sack of beans, I just gave up and sat down, watching the stack grow, in wonder and amazement. Doug dumped several cardboard cartons into my lap and suggested that I had better start practicing. Bull Durham. Well, I might have to do a lot of things, but I would not be smoking that filthy stuff! I pushed the lot onto the floor with disdain, and kicked it under the table.

Two hours later, the grub, as they called it, was unloaded. I got up enough courage to inquire just where we were to put it all. Doug's father smiled and said to wait. In they came, carrying a large plank, and proceeded to hoist it up onto the overhead beams. In all, seven planks were placed above our heads, and the grub stacked atop. I watched my picture of a cozy cabin evaporate into a picture of a cozy larder—complete with sides of bacon and hams hanging down to smack the careless head. As if that wasn't enough, the meat had to hang directly in front of the only window with a view, so the circulating air could keep the meat fresh, they said. Ha! If it was drafts of air they needed, virtually anyplace in the cabin would have done fine. I made up my mind to rearrange when they were gone.

Ma, in the meantime, had been holding David and talking to Dougie. She asked me where I was going to hang my clothesline. I realized with dismay that I hadn't even thought about doing laundry—not just our clothes, but the diapers, diapers, and more diapers that would need washing every day. Out we went to look around. We strung up the clothesline from one corner of the cabin to a group of alders about fifty feet away, to be as close to the water supply as possible. But where to put the tubs and other washday accoutrements? We decided to level off a fallen log just beside the cabin. The washtubs were placed on top. This, then, was to be my laundry room.

After the folks left—not without yards and yards of advice as to this and that and the other thing—I went back to the work of arranging the cabin. My books went onto the too-narrow shelves made by the two-by-fours supporting the roof. I remembered the spacious bookcase, well filled, that I had left behind, and started figuring means of getting the rest of my books up there.

I did my first washing, and as I hung it on the line it looked as though it had never seen water, let alone soap. My back ached from the continuous bending, my wrists hurt from the wringing, and my hands—well, the knuckles were raw and bleeding. I sat down on the log and cried for myself in self-pity. Dougie came chugging up (for he was, so he told me, a truck just then), peered at my red eyes, and said in a surprised, sympathetic voice, "Did you fall down, too, Mommy?"

"Yes dear, I did fall down into a mire, something you wouldn't understand, but now I'm up again, and see? I'm not even scratched!" I wiped my eyes and stood up, determined that if I must give way to self-pity, it had better be in solitude, rather than in front of Doug or the children.

David had fallen asleep in his bassinet, placed atop a tree stump in a sea of things placed atop tree stumps. A precious whole little life, right in amongst grimy tools, wash tubs, and other inconsequentials. He seemed to be sleeping soundly. Whether it was the fresh air, or that I simply couldn't pay as much attention to him, I didn't know.

There was nothing else I could do to decorate the cabin without spending money. And money was something I didn't have. As soon as possible, I would send for the mail order catalogue, and then, too, I could write a letter to my mother telling her of the things that I would like to have—cretonne fabric for the windows, a couple of India prints—and above all, I needed a cookbook!

Wash done, baby asleep, toddler engaged, I stood staring up at the mountains surrounding me. They looked so unfriendly. I felt like a prisoner.

Chapter 4
Summer, 1944: Dave

Fishing in nearby Pleasant Creek was a favorite pastime. It's hard to describe just how pristine and beautiful that little stream was. In all of the time we spent there, we never saw a footprint or gum wrapper or any evidence whatsoever of another human being. It was small enough to easily wade or jump from rock to rock, and there were long stretches of shallow water, followed by a series of pools and miniature falls. It was about a mile from the cabin to the creek, and then maybe another quarter-mile up to our favorite fishing hole, which we creatively named the Three Pools: just like fast food drinks, there was a small one, a medium, and a large. Beautiful tiger lilies bloomed at the base of the big pool every summer.

Our fishing rods were freshly cut, six-foot willow branches. We'd tie a six- or eight-foot length of monofilament line to the end, and then wind it around until only a short piece remained. To this we tied a hook.

The day before a fishing trip was for bait gathering. Worms were in short supply, so our favorite was live grasshoppers, which we kept in an old green Prince Albert tobacco can with holes punched in the top. Catching grasshoppers is not easy work, and we'd need at least fifteen to twenty for each of us. Experience proved that the best method was to walk side by side very slowly, with a hat in one hand. We'd watch where one in particular landed. Whichever of us was closest then slowly got down on hands and knees, and inched forward, waiting for it to jump again. As soon as it did, down came

The haul after one of our fishing trips.

the hat. Holding it firmly to the ground with one hand, we'd slide the other hand underneath and feel for signs of life. Taking the bugs alive was critical; a moving, twitching grasshopper was much more appealing to a fish than a dead one.

Before the sun hit the cabin the next morning we'd be gone, peanut butter and jam sandwiches and other sundries in our packs.

We'd fish all day nonstop, leap-frogging each other as we worked our way upstream. We both had small canvas creels slung over our shoulders to keep the little fish we caught. The trip home was delayed as long as possible, until the sun had been off the water for a while. Then one of us would begin running down the middle of the creek, hopping from rock to rock, with the other in hot pursuit. It seems we always got back to the cabin just as darkness was falling, so cleaning the fish had to be done by flashlight.

Fried trout for breakfast was a real treat. Mom would dip the fish in flour before they hit hot butter in the frying pan. We became experts at stripping out the bones and finishing a whole fish in a bite or two. They weren't very big, but twenty or thirty was enough for everyone.

On the hottest days, we'd hike up to Three Pools to swim in the middle pool. Well, actually, to say we swam much is misleading. It was perfect in every way except for the ice-cold temperature. We'd screw up our courage and then jump in. Instant paralysis of breathing mechanisms ensued; you'd scramble as fast as you could to get out and find a nice warm rock to sit on.

###

One morning, we talked Dad into going fishing with us. That time of year, the ticks were out in force, so as we pushed our way through the bush, we'd stop periodically for body checks. This of course was before anyone knew about Lyme Disease, but ticks were still nasty little bugs that would attach themselves and suck your blood, and that was enough for us to be on the lookout for them. We'd all strip to the waist or below and check for the small, spidery-looking little critters. It was unusual to not find at least one on each inspection. Ticks seemed to like soft tissue: under your arms, belt lines, and the groin area.

Doug and me, trying to stay cool and out of trouble.

We had begun fishing the Three Pools, with Dad standing eight feet or so above Doug and I, who were fishing the pool from below. Dad discovered a tick in one of his buttocks. It had already bored into the skin so he was faced with the task of getting it out. You didn't just pluck it off—the head was the part that burrowed into the skin, and pulling on the body risked leaving the head buried, which could lead to infection, or so we were told. The common method was to unscrew them—I think they bored in clockwise so you had to twist them counterclockwise. This procedure was preferably done by someone other than the victim.

So, there we were, in this beautiful spot, with the sun shining on Dad like a spotlight. Down came his pants, and declining our offers to help, he stood there with his white cheeks blinding us, trying to "unscrew" the damned tick. Doug and I didn't dare let our eyes meet; doing so would surely result in hysterical laughter and possibly a tumble into the creek. Not good fishing form. So we pretended to not watch as we fished, and sure enough, he finally got it out.

Ticks were also a constant torment to the dogs we had during our stay, Shep first, then Boots later. We'd check them often, mostly in the evenings as the family sat around the stove reading. Doug and I would delight in finding a tick we'd missed before that was now gorged with blood and the size of a small pea. We'd unscrew it and gently drop it on the hot stove. It would sit there for a moment, start to hop around and then, "pop"—it was gone. More of the simple entertainment made possible by mountain life.

Our location on the side of a canyon made a perfect spot for another classic boyhood pastime: sledding. What wasn't so classic was that for us, it was a summertime sport. A little-known fact is that slick madrona tree leaves make a dandy substitute for snow. Find a relatively open, steep slope covered with such leaves, flatten a cardboard box, and you're pretty much set for the afternoon.

We took turns flying down the hill on our cardboard sleds liked greased lightening. It was several hundred feet to the bottom, where Harris Creek trickled right next to the cabin, and we yelled at the top of our lungs the whole way down. Then we'd crawl back up the steep hill and toss the cardboard to the next rider, strategizing along the way how to go faster and farther next time.

We got pretty cocky about our skills "driving" a cardboard luge, and one afternoon, as I sat at the top mapping out my run, I decided on a slight but risky shift to the right. It would take me onto fresh leaves, but more importantly, the look of the run had a high fright factor and would definitely get my big brother's attention.

It was a gutsy call that paid off in new speed records and high drama, as, near the bottom, still waving and screaming, I went sailing smack into a yellow-jacket nest. You probably won't be surprised to learn that these industrious insects are also inordinately unforgiving. That run remains my most memorable sled ride ever—in any season.

A full load on the sled.

Chapter 5
Fall, 1933: Louise

The cabin was settled to the best of my ability. There were visions of how nice I could make it look with just a little money and the help of the mail-order stores—but alas! There just wasn't anything to spare for those sorts of things. We had $20 a month on which to live. That had to cover everything—gas for the truck, drugs as needed, stamps and other sundry articles, as well as food.

I began to look about me, wanting to see something of the country and the people around us. With the acquisition of a rat-tailed spaniel, Duke by name, I found courage to go out a bit after the children were in bed, with their dad there to watch over them. Although it was a six-mile trip to get the mail, the longing for word from home, family, and friends soon sent me, with a lantern and Duke, along the many long, lonely miles to the mailbox. The unearthly silence of the mountains at night draped a clammy blanket over me, and for a long time I walked with my breath coming in gasps. I held it to listen— what for, I don't know. The eerie light of the kerosene lantern threw shadows that caused me to stop and stare into the darkness ahead . . . NEVER behind! My heart beat loud enough, I am sure, to warn anything that might be near. Duke, being a bird dog, was off into the close-growing brush at the first sound, or the scent of some living creature. I would stand in the middle of the trail and call persuasively, "Duke . . . come on Duke . . . please, Duke . . . come on back." Then he would appear, invariably startling me. What relief when I finally reached the mailbox, and what disappointment if there should not be a single letter! I only managed to get down two or three times a week, so it wasn't very often that my journey went unrewarded.

It's not until one goes into an alien country, or away into the far-off places, that one appreciates the talents of a real correspondent. Out of my welter of city friends came at least three steady writers, pen pals who wrote of things besides their health and the latest jokes, or the weather conditions. What a jewel, the writer who can speak with pen as though he or she were there talking to you! There is also surprising delight in discovering a writer in someone with whom you have had only a passing acquaintance. I found one such person in a friend who is deaf. What grand letters this person wrote. Our world of letters opened up a new experience. I even took a correspondence course, and in the professor who corrected my lessons I found a sympathetic friend as well as a critic—and yet today, if I were to meet this person on the street, I would not recognize her.

My mother managed to send us a package at least once a month, and how we all looked forward to those packages! Some weighed as much as sixty pounds. I carried a gunnysack with me when going to the mailbox, just in case one of her packages arrived. I would haul the box in the sack as far as our nearest neighbors. There, I would open it to the admiring circle of eyes that always gathered to "ooh" and "ah" at such things as fresh pineapple, coconut, lettuce, carrots, and celery. From the package, I would transfer those things that I felt I could not leave behind, even until the next day. Over my shoulder would go the gunnysack filled to the brim with magazines, foodstuffs, and cigarettes—oh, those tailor-made cigarettes! How grand they were. The children always got the same manner of toy: a small rubber automobile, or a box of crayons. Doug and I would sit up until all hours, reading— of all things—the funny papers! But, when one hasn't seen a funny paper for months—well, I make no claim to being intellectual and I do enjoy the funny papers—even the Katzenjammer Kids.

I rebelled at first at the confining limits of my new life. Gradually, I came to look to myself and my husband for entertainment. I found old authors, and made new acquaintances amongst the latest writers via the Oregon State Library. Their mail order system of taking *out books hasn't been praised half enough to my way of thinking.*

The mountains cultivated a sense of philosophy, and a chance for introspection. During those years spent in the mountains, I looked within myself, and like a desk full of pigeonholes, I found that my mind was stuffed with ideas that needed scrapping, like old papers gathered over a period of years.

###

It was October and the woods were beautiful in crashing reds and yellows. The air was snappy, but we didn't worry. Our nearest neighbors some miles away were two dear bachelors, ex-sourdoughs and partners for thirty-five years. They were both named Charlie so I naturally called them the Charlies. They made vague excuses to call upon us, but the conversation always came around to the subject of wood. When were we going to get our wood in? Well, we didn't exactly know, we said, and besides, it seemed like there was a lot of potential fire tender just lying around. Finally, they allowed as how they thought that 200-foot fir outside was just a mite too close to the cabin. First heavy snowfall or wind might bring it down, and there was no telling just which way it might fall . . . Consequently, we found ourselves with oodles of wood, and no woodshed. The Charlies gave us directions on to how to build a woodshed, and Doug got started. The big difficulty was that we had plenty of firewood—but no lumber for building. Eventually, we built the shed out of slabs of bark with saplings for support. Really, it was a parody of woodsheds—it slanted in one direction, and sagged in another. Then we found, much to our disgust, that we had to bend over to even get inside. As a final insult, when the rains began, it became clear that whatever we had built, it wasn't a shed to protect firewood—all the wood was wet.

Along with my housewifely duties, I also had a baby to care for. The daily washing was a nightmare—water to carry, fires to make, endless scrubbing that never seemed to get the dinginess out. Then, the biggest problem of all: trying to get those clothes dry! Our little cabin resembled a Chinese laundry. Clothes festooned the place, and with every move, one came in contact with clammy diapers, woolly sleepers, Doug's long underwear, my foundations, or little Dougie's many things—he managed to get wet throughout three or four times a day.

David was soon going to be in need of a highchair, and it seemed the only way he would get it would be for Doug to build it. Doug had never built anything in his life except birdhouses and such. You should have seen the highchair he constructed—it looked like a Rube Goldberg contraption. Then David outgrew his wicker basket, and a crib was in order. This was made from alder saplings and two-by-fours. It was by no means a work of art, but it served its purpose of keeping the little monkey within a confined space.

Someone back home had the bright idea of sending me a swing for David, one of those canvas things that balances on a spring. Every time my back was turned, he managed to work himself into such a fever pitch of bouncing that the swing would turn him upside down. He would yell, and I would turn around to find him spinning like a top, on his head!

The rains persisted in a steady downpour for nights and days on end. Evenings were wells of stillness broken only by the steady hammering on the tar-paper roof. I sat night after night with nothing to read, and thought I should go berserk if that rhythm did not stop. I sat staring until the shock of encroaching cold came upon me and I realized that the teakettle had stopped its wheezy song—notification that the fire in the little sheet-iron stove had gone out.

I daydreamed of a spell during the summer when it had been 100 degrees in the shade for multiple days. A crew had been on the place, logging cedar. I had cooked for them on a wood and coal stove, and oh, how hot it had been in that tiny cabin! At the end of the day, a cool, washing wind would begin to sway the trees. After the children *were in bed, I would sit out on the door stoop with Duke beside me, take deep breaths of the breeze, and try to smooth out the wrinkles in my nerves. Now in the drippy, dreary grey, I longed for those spells on the stoop, daylight stretching far into evening, breathing the cool, dry air.*

Amongst the things I learned during the fall rains was how to roll cigarettes by hand. I swore at first that I would quit smoking rather than learn to roll my own, but the habit was well entrenched. I began by experimenting. Those first cigarettes were a joke, they didn't stay together and I would wind up with tobacco in my mouth instead of in the cigarette. It took many months of practice before I could roll one that I could smoke in public.

To the mountain people, I was a hussy because I smoked cigarettes. Before I left, I had a try at the art of "chewin' tobaccy," which was the preferred method for both men and women. I had a horrible toothache and it was thirty-six miles to the dentist. At someone's suggestion, I finally resorted to a piece of tobacco held against my aching tooth. It did stop the ache, but the nausea it caused was almost as bad. No one told me I shouldn't swallow the awful stuff! To this day, my husband delights in telling a few select people that I can and have chewed.

Dusk in the fall mountains came in purples and greys. The birds would create quite a flutter before settling in for the night. My favorite was the wood thrush, which had a peculiar call just at dusk and dawn. It was a questioning, restless cry—I often wished I could give my mind relief from the monotony with just some such cry. People do get queer notions.

###

I got quite a thrill out of reading cookbooks. I had managed to obtain a few, and recipes for such outlandish impossibilities as Lobster à la Newburgh made my mouth water as though someone had passed a dish of pickles under my nose. I read these recipes with all the zest that most people read a novel. Pictures of fancy entrées were fascinating, and I tried to copy those that didn't call for too many ingredients. I recall attempting a rather intricate biscuit recipe, the result of which turned out to resemble not so much biscuits, but rather smooth, water-worn rocks, fresh from the creek. I threw them to the chickens, who refused to eat them.

In fact, as much as I loved reading cookbooks, the actual cooking was a constant perplexity to me. I had never been good in the kitchen, and found myself even struggling with our daily basics, most of which included beans.

My first attempt at baking bread turned into a farce. The yeast that had been packed in was evidently not quite fresh. At any rate, I kneaded and kneaded, and KNEADED—until finally, the bread was in lovely rounded loaves and ready for the oven. I called Doug to see the result of my labors. Impressed, he responded, "Well, I hope they taste as good as they look." It turned out to be an overly optimistic wish. Oh, that bread! Two lovely, golden brown bricks! Our cabin door was made of planking, and braced with two-by-fours. Doug pushed the door back and put one loaf of bread against it. Nothing moved. That bread doorstop worked as if it had been made of pure iron. I will never live that down. My brick bread has become part of family lore. In time, I did learn to make fairly palatable bread, but nothing to equal the quality of my grandmother's.

Of course, even the best of chefs would have had a rough time with my provisions and kitchen. All of my ingenuity was called to bear to put tasty, nutritious food on the table. During the winter months we hardly ever saw fresh vegetables, unless we received a package from Mother or were the beneficiaries of some carrots or cabbage from a neighbor's cellar. I did learn to make some pretty mean soups and stews. My first attempt was watery and tasteless. But then I stumbled onto the secret: slow, long cooking. Aha!

My success with stews spurred me on to more ambitious heights. Over time, I learned to can, putting up jellies and jams, ketchups and relishes. The first time I made jelly, I used crab apples, and unless the reader happens to be familiar with these miniature replicas of real apples, they can hardly know the labor necessary to gain a few glasses of lovely amber jelly. Have you ever canned venison? One of our bachelor neighbors told me to let the deer meat hang for about a week, and then soak it in vinegar all night. The longer it hangs in a cool place, the better it will be; more tender and moist. And the vinegar soak is crucial.

Eventually, I also learned many shortcuts to good food, such as how to bake a decent cake with only one egg—or none. Those old bachelors could make the best bread and pancakes from sourdough: a terrible-looking mess kept in a stone jar. When I first heard of it, I had only known of people called sourdoughs; I quickly realized where they had gotten the moniker—sourdough was what the miners had used to make bread and biscuits, and so had been given the nickname. The trick of using this concoction is to keep adding flour, and about once or twice a month, a tiny pinch of yeast. The old miners obligingly gave me a sourdough "start." But, I kept forgetting to "feed" it. Consequently, my sourdough hotcakes were absolutely terrible. I gave up, but most all of the people in the mountains, particularly the bachelors, used sourdough for supplying their tables with bread and hotcakes. I tried to convince them that making fresh batter every morning was far easier, and just as good, but they could never be converted to my way of modern cookery.

Eggs presented a particular difficulty. We went to town maybe once a month; during the winter it might be many months before we saw a store. For a long time we used powdered eggs. It may not sound so bad, but just try eating wilted scrambled eggs and omelets time after time after time. I'll venture you might find yourself yearning for a dish of nice eggs, fried in butter, with the whites pale white and the yokes a lovely golden shade. Our neighbors—those within seven or eight miles—had chickens, but during the winter months the hens go through a period of molting and the cold delays laying.

After a while, though, a hen was given to us. I was thrilled at the idea of having an egg every day. We built quite a good-sized hen house, and when that hen went to roost at night she was completely lost within it. She refused to lay in the house we built. I finally found her nest after much "Sherlocking." It was under the house—in a box—in a space about six inches high. So there I would stand in the cabin, waiting for the signal that she had done her duty. Then I would rush out and crawl under the house! Having decent baked goods on the menu depended upon this one hen and her temperamental laying.

One day, late in the fall, it had been snowing for two solid weeks and I decided to go down to our nearest neighbors and ask to buy a dozen eggs. I dressed warmly and started out. It is an experience worth trying, that of carrying a dozen eggs in a paper sack, with the snow coming down and making the paper sack so moist it threatens to disintegrate. I needed those eggs, and carried them as if they were gold nuggets. Alas, just as I stepped upon a log to cross the creek, the snow slid off, and I lit in the creek. I sat there in the icy water, the tears rolling down my cheeks as I gazed upon the gooey yellow mass that rose from my lap to float off down the stream. There went all of the cakes and puddings I had planned for.

Another time, a neighbor family had contracted to clear an acre or two for a mining company. The mother of the family came down with what I diagnosed as flu, but they insisted was the megrims and the grippe. They hiked up and asked if I would be neighborly and come for just a few days to help out with the cooking for the family and the men they had hired to help. Up there, that was what people did, so I obligingly took the baby, packed a few things, and went down to help. I have never seen anyone eat like those men ate! I've since had nightmares of the dozens of loaves of bread and huge pots of beans I was expected to produce. I found that I had to count on one loaf of bread for each person at every meal. The quantity of beans, cakes, puddings, eggs, bacon, pies, and rolls I made at that house was astonishing. All of the family names were biblical, and it was fitting because they ate in biblical proportions. At home, I was accomplishing a great deal when I made three loaves of bread at a time. There, I had to make six times that for each meal! Breakfast was a gargantuan feast compared to my city idea of breakfast, which was fruit, coffee, and once in a blue

Mom swinging a wood-splitting maul for show; it was probably at least six pounds.

moon, a boiled egg. Their breakfast menu included at least three eggs per person, a platter of fried ham or bacon, a huge pot of mush (the oatmeal variety), several baking pans of biscuits, and several frying pans of cream gravy. Fruit seldom graced the breakfast table. Then, to top off the meal, pitchers of milk warm from the barns or hot, bitter coffee. Jams and jellies were always on the board in several varieties. This was a spectacle I had never seen before, let alone prepared.

To get this meal on the table by 6 a.m. (at the very latest), I had to rise in the wee small hours before dawn. The men of the household seldom bothered to bring in wood, let alone chop any. This business of getting up, starting fires (with the wood box always empty) and putting a gigantic meal on the table completely overwhelmed my powers of ingenuity. And, to think that the women of these mountain families took it all for granted! No wonder the lady of the house wasn't feeling well! I lasted two days, and then, thanks be to God, Doug came down to take me home, for Dougie was coming down with a fever. The little cabin had never looked quite so good to me as it did that afternoon, when I happily came back to the simple task of providing meals for just three people and a baby—none with a Rabelaisian appetite.

Chapter 6
Fall, 1944: Dave

Summer wound down and I dreaded the demise of my freedom. My relationship with school was, to say the least, a difficult one, and my sixth grade at the small elementary school in Wimer was a lackluster continuation of my five previous years. I was a terrible student, and routinely got into trouble. I was smart enough, and my teacher Mrs. Jensen tried her best, but I had absolutely no interest in verbs or fractions or whatever I was supposed to be storing away in my brain. I remember staring longingly out the window at the high mountains to the west, wishing I was there, exploring the hidden caves and secret places.

Eventually, Mom's love of reading would rub off on me, making up for some of what I had missed in school. I wish my patient teachers could have known that I would achieve a modicum of success, and that while I still couldn't tell a noun from an adverb nor understand Algebra 101, I would somehow eventually secure both a bachelor's and a master's degree.

But that would all come long after sixth grade.

When school let out, I'd get on the yellow school bus. Doug was already on board, having started in Rogue River. The bus was full at first, but would thin out as we wound our way up the curvy gravel road. Ultimately, we came to the last row of mailboxes, where the bus would turn around and head back to Wimer. At this point, it was just Doug, the driver, and me. We'd say goodbye, check the mailbox, and head up the road to home. (In the mornings, the last thing Mom would say as we headed down

70

the hill in the dark was, "Don't forget the mail!")

A half-mile or so toward home, we would make a stop at the Johnson place, an authentic log cabin where Abe (Mr. "White Lightening") and his sister Babe lived. The Johnsons made their living logging. Yes, she was a logger, too; built like a man, with close-cropped blond hair. Babe was naturally good-natured and when she smiled, which was a lot, it disclosed large gaps where several front teeth had once been. Babe "chewed," and when it came to spitting, she was as good as any man.

We could tell she welcomed our daily visits, insisting we come in and take home fresh-baked rolls or bread. There's nothing like just-out-of-the-oven bread. She'd wrap some for us to take home, then cut a thick slice for each of us, slather it with homemade butter and strawberry jam. Heaven. Once, the jam jar was almost empty and to get out the last bit, she ran her finger around the jar, spread it on the slices, licked her finger, then once again went back in the jar with the same finger for that final dollop. Doug's eyes met mine. We thanked her for the loaf to take home, but as soon as we were our of sight of the cabin, we looked at each other, burst out laughing, and sailed the finger-licking-good slices of bread off into the brush for some woodland creature to enjoy.

While talking to Abe one day, perhaps waiting for our treat before continuing the trek home, he regaled us with the story of a big Indian fight that had occurred nearby, on the aptly named Battle Mountain. As Abe described the clash, he motioned for us to follow him outside to the back porch. Reaching under the porch, he pulled out an old apple crate. It was overflowing with arrowheads, old rifle balls, and other remnants of the skirmish, fueling our imaginations and creating rich story lines for subsequent reenactments.

The fall rains began and changed everything. Jutting up behind us were high mountain ridges, which provided shade in the summer but made for dreary, misty gloom in the shortening days of autumn. Water dripped off the trees. Low overhanging clouds cast shadows over the mountain. Outside activity was limited to keeping the wood box full and seeing to our animals. During breaks in the weather, we'd tend to outside chores such as patching a roof leak. Inside, we helped Mom with laundry and did our homework.

One of my school friends that year invited me to visit their farm up on Evans Creek. Pleasant Creek was a tributary of the larger Evans Creek. He mentioned something about steelhead fishing, which got me very excited.

As my friend's dad drove us up the road that ran along Evans Creek, we came to a section of uniformly shallow water, with lots of sand and small gravel.

We slowed way down and my friend's father watched the stream intently. Suddenly, he hit the breaks and pointed. "There they are!" he exclaimed, with the anticipation of a hawk spotting a field mouse. We jumped out of the truck and I looked for his fishing rod. Instead, he grabbed a .30-30 rifle from the back window rack. Raising the gun to his shoulder, he took aim at the river. Just as I was trying to wrap my head around what was going on, the crack! crack! crack! of the rifle echoed back and forth across the creek. He lowered his rifle. Nobody did or said anything. After a minute or so, the fish hunter climbed back in the cab and re-racked his gun; we followed. I later learned that the local method of steelheading was to shoot at the fish—not hitting, but stunning them. The fish would then float to the surface, paralyzed, and you'd simply pluck them out of the water. I was simultaneously horrified and fascinated by this approach, having been raised as a willow-pole man, and so was both relieved and slightly disappointed when the trip ended with a bang but no fish.

###

On a typical school day, Dad would be up and building a

fire at 5 a.m. The sound of the crackling fire usually woke Doug and me. Breakfast was what we call oatmeal today, but we knew it as mush. It was hot and if you added some raisins, brown sugar, and canned milk, it wasn't half bad.

Mom devised an ingenious and particularly cruel means by which to get us up and fed, our chickens and rabbits tended, and our butts out the door for school. It was my first practical encounter with the concept of incentives. The rule was, the last one to get back from taking care of his animals had to clean the mush pan. Now, oatmeal is one name for mush—an alternate might be concrete, when it's cooked onto the insides of a pot. And to clean this mess from the pan, you had to go out the back door and over to the flume where the water poured like a small waterfall from the wooden "V" Dad had built. All the while, the rain was trickling down your back while you scrubbed, then checked with the flashlight (which you held in your teeth), scrubbed some more, and finally raced back to the cabin to get out of the rain. So, while we lingered in bed as long as possible, as soon as Mom yelled that breakfast was on, we would spring from our beds, scramble into our jeans and shirts, race into the kitchen, wolf down the mush, throw on our jackets, tear out the front door and sprint down the hill to the chicken coop and rabbit hutches—all the while pacing ourselves, according to how the other seemed to be getting along that morning. Then it was a race to the death back up the hill, bursting through the door. On many a morning we could have used instant replay.

###

The fall of 1944 was the beginning of my brother's long-term love affair with basketball. On his way to work early each weekday, Dad would drop Doug off at the high school in Rogue River, where he was in the ninth grade. He was very small for his age, not even five feet tall. The school was not officially open at that time of the morning, but a nice janitor would let him in to shoot baskets. He made the ninth grade team and was over the moon.

Fate and the germ world intervened at a most inopportune time that fall, though. On the day of the big game against arch rival Illinois Valley, Doug came down with a bad cold. Mom and Dad told him he'd have to stay home. Doug was crushed; he'd been told he would be a starter. But Dad was firm. Doug had what we now call a meltdown—a screaming, crying tantrum the likes of which I'd never seen. At one point I thought they were going to have to physically restrain him from bolting out the door and down the road to get to that game. He finally calmed down, but stayed livid for days.

Basketball became a major part of his life. When we moved back to Grants Pass the next year, he continued to improve and ultimately was one of the best basketball handlers to ever play at Grants Pass High. Six feet tall when he graduated, he earned a scholarship to what is now Portland State University and later Gonzaga University. He finished his basketball career playing for a Eugene AAU team that made it to the national playoff tournament in Denver in 1953. Long before the NBA, these were the professional basketball teams of the time. His team took fourth and Doug won the distinction of being selected Most Promising Young Player at the tournament.

My interest in sports began that year as well, when I won my first foot race at school. I would also do well later in high school, running track and playing on the Oregon State High School Championship football team. Eventually I was offered full-ride scholarships to several colleges, and wisely accepted one to run track at the University of Oregon for the renowned coach Bill Bowerman.

During the first cabin stay in the '30s, Dad's plan for

making a living had included striking it rich mining for gold. An entry in one of Mom's journals mentions him coming home with $20 in small nuggets and bits and pieces they called "gold dust." It's not entirely clear how his plan "panned out," but it's pretty clear the mother lode he was hoping to find never materialized.

Whatever Dad's involvement with prospecting, he certainly wouldn't have been the first to look to "them thar hills" with a glint in his eye. Southern Oregon's history as a gold-mining mecca is a rich one. From the mid-1800s to early in the twentieth century, gold mining was the region's primary economy. But as World War II began, the price of gold per ounce was fixed at $35 an ounce, and almost all mining came to a sudden standstill. (In the last few years, the price of gold has risen to over $1,000 an ounce— at times, well over). Reminders of mining operations past were everywhere around us at the cabin, and the seductive lore was a source of constant fascination, though much of what had been left in the fever's wake was ugly, with little mind to the land or what destruction the extraction methods had wrought.

In the evolutionary life of gold mining, there were several periods and prevailing methods. Water—lots of it—was essential to all but the last and most recent of gold mining methods. This latter technique is called "hardrock" and involves digging deep tunnels into mountains, looking for a vein or at least gold-bearing quartz. The original road up to the cabin had been built to reach just such a hardrock mine, way up on the mountain behind the cabin. While hiking past that open mine shaft with Dad one day, he told us to not explore such places, warning in his sternest voice, "That's where rattlesnakes hang out."

Panning was the first and easiest process. It's an iconic picture: the grizzled prospector, kneeling near a small creek, swirling a shallow metal bowl. Streambed material fills the bottom of the pan; the swirling is to skim off the lighter dirt and gravel, while allowing heavier pieces that have washed down the stream (hopefully gold) to settle in the bottom of the pan.

A step up from panning was a clever technological advance called a rocker. It was something of a crude baby cradle with a screen filter and lower tray, placed directly in the stream and then shoveled full of dirt. It was rocked back and forth, again with the heavier materials falling to the bottom tray, to be removed and panned. It allowed the miner to work through more material, faster.

The next feat of mining ingenuity, a sluice, required additional manpower. Parallel to the stream, a wooden trough was built, maybe two feet wide by three feet deep and extending from top to bottom perhaps as long as twenty yards. Inside the wooden trough, small wooden steps called "cleats" were installed—they were maybe two inches high. At the top of the sluice was a gate mechanism to stop and start the flow of water. When open, the gate would allow the stream to be diverted into the trough, creating a flow of water down the trough, then back into the stream at the bottom end. The miners, as many as ten, would shovel dirt into the trough. Large rocks were washed down or picked out by the men. The cleats caught the smaller and heavier pieces. When the cleats were full, the top water gate would be closed and the miners would pan the material caught behind the cleats.

As you can imagine, the miners were always thinking of bigger and better ways to wash more water through more dirt. That's when things turned ugly. Gold fever leaves scarce room for thoughts of land conservation, and the result was "hydraulic" mining—an undertaking which amounted to fire hoses water-blasting entire hillsides. The force of the water would dislodge tons of dirt and rock, causing it (and often most of the hillside) to fall into waiting troughs below. When the cleats were full, their yields would be panned.

The trick with hydraulic mining was establishing enough water pressure to sufficiently blast the top several layers of earth off a hillside. Huge ditches or wood flumes had to be built upstream to carry the water downhill at such a pitch as to create the necessary pressure. The Charlies had employed this method of mining, and piles of the remnant pipes still sat rusting on what we called "the flats," the property where their cabin had been, a quarter-mile down the road from ours. In our wanderings, Doug and I would occasionally come upon these ditch/flume systems high up on a hill beside a stream.

In 1944-45 there remained huge areas along Pleasant Creek where countless piles of rocks served as monuments to man's quest for gold. These funny little eight-to-ten-foot-tall humps stood out in stark contrast to the untouched beauty of the surrounding woods.

The most spectacular example we saw of hydraulic mining's impact was on a section of land going cross-country from the cabin to the Three Pools. Heading downhill, we would be walking through pristine forest one moment, and the next, be at the edge of a dramatic vertical drop-off of approximately sixty feet. Peering down, the landscape below was a moonscape: a sun-baked, barren sheet of dirt and rock sparsely dotted with tiny islands of vegetation. The distance across this stripped stretch to the tree-shaded creek was only two hundred feet or so, but the contrast was breathtaking.

From the bottom looking up, it was like lines had been drawn down the hillside where the giant hoses had long ago stopped their insatiable hunger for dirt, and left the roots of the forest exposed. The overhang at the top could be as much as five feet, and we realized we should never go close to the edge when approaching from above.

Today, hydraulic mining is outlawed in most areas due to its devastating effects on natural terrain.

Chapter 7
Winter, 1933: Louise

One *fall morning, while going about my work, I heard the sound of far-off honking. I ran outside and sure enough, high in the sky was the beautiful "V" formation of a southbound flock of geese. Winter would soon be upon us, which meant an impassable creek, snow-blocked roads, and packing in anything that had to be replenished.*

All the little household tasks I had been putting off were immediately accomplished. The cabin roof was checked for leaks; the woodshed roof was braced; the henhouse mended. Saws and axes were oiled, and all but the small hand axe were stored away.

The grocery supply was assessed, and a long list made for the trip to town. Kerosene, gasoline, medicines, and all the heavy staples were purchased. We bought potatoes, sugar, flour, and coffee in hundred-pound bags. Still, we ran out of things that winter. There was at least one run for canned milk, purchased by the case and hauled in six miles on Doug's back. I'm sure there were other replacement necessities we had to pack in that I'm forgetting.

My auspicious initiation to getting a wood stove going (from our summer arrival) was an early indicator of my sad skills as a fire starter. It wasn't for lack of effort. First, the paper, if we had any, was wadded up in the firebox, then the kindling, then the large kindling, then the main firewood. Then—the match! It would all blaze up gloriously, my hopes would soar, and then . . . the flames would promptly die out. Another try—another failure. Finally, in desperation, I would traipse out to the woodshed and find a piece of pitchy pine. Almost always, that would do the trick. I watched Doug light fires over and over, and then copied his techniques exactly. But try as I might, my fires were never like his.

###

Short, cold, snowy days gave me time to ponder the lives of my valley neighbors. I should start any discussion of them by saying that in the end, my ties to these people and this place would become some of the strongest of my life. Yet it took me a long time to gain anything more than just a nodding acquaintance with the mountain folk. They are hard to get to know, though it was not difficult to become the center of conversation. It was queer; I could go six miles to get the mail and never see a soul, but the next day the valley would be buzzing: "That Mrs. Talbot, she went to the mailbox yistidy, and got so many letters, and she was dressed in sich and sich an outfit." It was uncanny the way the grapevine of gossip encircled that valley. As a newcomer, I was the focus of those hostile and invisible eyes. They all nodded to me, and some eventually spoke after six months or so.

And then it happened. Even though I was still a relative newcomer, I started to find myself staring in this same impassive way at a new person who came in a friendly manner to the mailbox. I heard myself speaking in the local dialect; saw myself taking on the same wary attitude.

As in all hill countries, we had plenty of characters. Perhaps my favorite was the storyteller; his fame spread far and wide. We heard the tale of the cyclone that blew the corn cob through a knot hole and shucked it; the one about the hunter who shot a deer in the head with a cherry seed bullet, then found the same deer a year later with a cherry tree growing from its head. These stories were repeated over and over, and every time with the same expressions and gestures. They never failed to draw a laugh.

There were also customs particular to this corner of the world that seemed as quirky as the people. For example, they had an odd way to designate different times of day. I once asked an old fellow, replete with droopy drawers and handlebar mustache, what the correct time was. He replied, "Well, it is nigh on to quarter-time." I found, after much inquiry (very discreetly, to be sure), that "quarter-time" was about nine o'clock in the morning, "half-time" was twelve noon, "three-quarters-time" was meant to denote three o'clock, and six o'clock was "whole time." I have never found any other place that told time in this manner.

I found the moral codes strict on some trivial matters, lax in things I had been taught were important.

There was a Mr. Lippman, a tall, thin man who had raised a huge family, and whose wife had given up the ghost after the thirteenth child. These children each grew up, only to leave home as quickly as possible. He lived alone in a little house on a poor piece of land. I heard, after a time, rumors about him and his housekeeper, but didn't think anything of it until one day when I met them together. I was astonished to see a young woman in her mid-twenties. She was dressed in a pair of green velvet lounging pajamas and a brown sport coat. Mr. Lippman's grey handlebar moustache positively bristled with antagonism as they passed me—he being one of the gossipers, now with the tables turned.

She eventually left, and other housekeepers came and went as well. Then one day, Mr. Lippman announced to the world that he was engaged, and his fiancée was coming by train from Chicago. The whole valley was abuzz at the news, and speculation was rampant. Quite suddenly, Mr. Lippman's fiancée was there, and he announced that they were married! The news got around that they had met through the medium of a matrimonial magazine. I think it was Heart and Help, or something to that effect. It wasn't but about two weeks when Mr. Lippman appeared at the mailbox—alone again! No one dared ask questions, for he looked quite like he wouldn't take kindly to inquiries. A little later, we found that Mr. Lippman's fiancée, or wife, had left him. Then, a little later it came out that they hadn't been married at *all. She was gone, but not forgotten—he was being sued by her for breach of promise! This touch of worldliness tickled my sense of humor. The general opinion of the valley was that he certainly had it coming to him. Then, the poor man went away. Some weeks later, he appeared again at the mailbox. Slowly but surely, the news leaked that he had settled with her out of court for some monetary amount. One would think that this would have been a lesson to the lanky Lothario, but within a couple of weeks, he had another housekeeper!*

Another bachelor up there I named Ichabod Crane, for he sorely reminded me of Irving's character. He was quite a Don Juan, to his way of thinking. Indeed, several women in the area admitted to me of succumbing to his apparent charms. I was as friendly toward him as I was to anyone, but did not share the other women's fascination. Poor Ichabod mistook my courtesy for flirtation, and took things further than he should have, for I slapped his face, read him the riot act, and sent him packing.

I meant to not mention his little act, but soon I heard gossip to the effect that I had not rejected but welcomed his advances! Apparently hell hath no fury like a man scorned. I quickly let the truth of the matter be known, and soon Ichabod found himself the laughing stock of the group that gathered at the mailbox. Of course I told Doug, and he sent word to Ichabod that the next time they met . . . ! Ichabod was a tall, long, lean fellow, and my husband is not any of those things, so it was quite comic to see the way Ichabod went out of his way to avoid a meeting with my Doug. As for Ichabod—he could never look me in the eye again, and if he met me on the road to the mailbox, he crossed the road to the other side as though I were something quite dangerous.

One old chap, for whom I felt great sympathy, was Mr. Fenn. When we first arrived, his wife had just been taken to the county hospital, about sixty miles away. The poor old fellow had no way of getting there himself. So word went around that if anyone was going to town, would they please take Mr. Fenn (the wife was in for quite a stretch). On one of our trips, he came along, and we heard the story of how he happened to come to this country.

He and his wife had bought the land sight unseen while living in the Midwest. They were told that it was timberland (and so it was), that a sawmill was being built in the valley, and that they would share in the natural wealth of the area. When they arrived, they put up a log cabin made of peeled and hand-adzed logs, with the prevalent red adobe for chinking. They had planned, of course, to build a real house when the promised sawmill went up. But as they soon discovered, a mill was nowhere in the offing. So, on the Fenn family went. Their children had grown up in that small, crude cabin, and like all of the valley's offspring, if they had any ambition at all, had left for better prospects elsewhere. The old couple had carried on as best they could. Neighbors helped them harvest their hay, and with other farming needs. When Mrs. Fenn had finally taken to her bed, the neighbors had cared for her. And when she finally required hospitalization, it was a terrible wrench for the couple. They had never been a night apart, in all their married years.

Mrs. Fenn eventually died. I saw the notice on the pole at the postboxes. The entire community was invited to the funeral. Everyone was reading the obituary, and all the women were talking about what they would wear. I was shocked—one would have thought they were going to the theatre, instead of a funeral. The Hewitts planned on attending, and were figuring out where they could get a battery for their old car. Driving in general was an issue in these parts—in Oregon at the time, your auto license fee was determined by how much your car weighed. Consequently, few people could afford to buy a license each year. So, when they had to go to town, they took backstreets, parked their cars out of the way, and walked into the business district.

Well, the Hewitts were going, and the plans were all neatly made—a lunch would be put up, and those neighbors who were not fortunate enough to own a car would go along with them (as many as could fit, at least).

When we arrived at the Hewitts to be part of the entourage (we were taking our own car, but were going to caravan together), I found their youngest child Betty, a girl of ten, in tears because she couldn't go to the funeral. I was taken aback, and asked why in the world she wanted to go to a funeral so badly. Then it all came out—whenever the family went anywhere in the car, Betty was always left at home because someone had to see that the chickens were fed and locked up and the cows were brought in from pasture. Betty never got to go anywhere, so she had her own reasons to be sad about the funeral, though they had nothing to do with Mrs. Fenn.

We all started out for town, but had gone only about a mile when something went wrong with the Hewitts' car. They were almost in front of the Alstons', who were not going to the funeral. So, out they piled: Hewitts, neighbors, flowers, and lunch, all into the Alstons' small house.

We went on to the funeral, and when I next saw them, Mrs. Hewitt reported, "Well, it was a great disappointment not to be able to see Mrs. Fenn laid to rest, but then, we did have a grand dinner with the Alstons." The flowers were eventually chucked out the back door for the chickens to root through.

A funeral was never allowed to hold up the daily ritual of living. If a woman's husband died, he was laid out and buried quite promptly. No one up there had a hired hand, so it was up to the widow to, in the slang of the day, "make it snappy." She had the cows to bring in and feed, milk, and bed down for the night. I never could get over this impressive fact, that the cows and stock always had to be brought in and fed, even if the world was coming to an end.

There was one reigning family in the area, the Coles. It was said in the valley that "you couldn't kick a hound dog without kicking a Cole." The original family had come from the Kentucky mountains and had been the valley's first settlers, then another branch of the same clan had joined them. These two families were the only residents for a good many years.

Consequently, there was quite a lot of intermarriage and this continued until other folks started moving into the area. This clan really was like royalty. The sheriff was a Cole, the postmaster was a Cole, and so on. Politics were just the means by which the Coles might *change things to suit their needs or whims. A new family did not stand a chance against them. Of course, the laws were antiquated, as might be expected. They hadn't been changed in generations and I once heard a Cole promise, "They ain't a'goin' to be changed, by heck."*

###

Christmas 1933 was something that even now, I do not like to recall. Not that the children went without anything, they really had plenty—but, we spent that Christmas with relatives, who supplied everything from the stockings on the mantel to all of Christmas morning's gifts, to the huge dinner. We were sent to bed with the other children, and Doug's family arranged the stockings and the gifts under the tree. I went to bed and lay there listening to the giggles and low whispers of tissue-wrapped gifts traveling from the hall closet to the front room. I thought my heart would break. Everyone jibed me the next morning for my long face, but outside of my husband, I don't think anyone realized why I just could not enter into the spirit of the day. It was with a bitter taste that I saw my first-born, Dougie, open a wagon that I had gazed upon with longing in the mail-order catalogue, and watched my baby David dissolve into smiles at the elephant made incongruously with pink dots. I kept reminding myself that I should be thankful that they could have these things, but how I ached to be the giver!

Chapter 8
Winter, 1945: Dave

Throughout the winter and well into spring—as long as Pleasant Creek was high and impassable by auto—coming and going from home included treks either to or from where we parked the car (a mile from the cabin), or to or from the school bus (an extra mile farther). While Doug got a ride to school with Dad in the mornings, I was left to make the two-mile trek to the bus, usually in the dark, often in snow. Heading out from home was downhill; coming home was a steep hike back.

We had stocked up as much as possible before the rains closed the road, but packing things in and out was still necessary for life's requirements: fresh food, clothes, kerosene, Mom's books,

Doug, Dad, Mom, and me, winter 1944.

and whatever we happened to be running low on—canned milk, toilet paper, rabbit pellets. We'd carry twenty- to thirty-pound packs and when you finally took them off you were left with the constant feeling of falling forward.

While it rained more than it snowed, I can well remember huffing and puffing up the hill through falling snow. We took turns breaking trail, pushing through the icy crust, the one in front holding the flashlight. What a welcome sight to finally come around the bend and see the lights of the cabin and the smoke from the chimney, and know we'd soon be warm.

Besides the arduousness of the trek in and out, we also had to contend with crossing Pleasant Creek at high water, or when it was snowy or icy, on foot and with a heavy pack. The only bridge was a fallen tree, maybe sixteen inches wide. Dad had flattened the top but left some of the larger branches as handholds.

After a big rain, sweet little Pleasant Creek turned into a raging torrent. The sight of the churning water below was frightening enough, but even worse was the sound. That volume of water has enormous force and could dislodge huge boulders. It was the sound of the rocks and boulders crashing along that made for such a massive roar. A slip would have likely meant death, either

Crossing Pleasant Creek in my Aunt Pat's Model A.

by falling trauma or hyperthermia, so it was always a slow-going, focused undertaking, especially so when the "bridge" sported a layer of snow or ice. When the log was slippery, Dad would go first then train his flashlight on our path as we inched across. "Don't pick up your feet," he'd admonish us. "Just slide them forward one at a time. And reach for the branch just ahead." It was always a relief to get to the other side.

One snowy evening, Dad parked the car just before the turnoff road to the cabin, and we gathered at the trunk to put on our Wellington boots, heavy jackets, and knit caps. After loading our packsacks and checking our flashlights, off we went, crunch, crunching through the snow. There was about two feet of snow on the ground, which got deeper as we climbed up the hill.

We finally made it to "the flats" and the two Charlies' cabin. We were pausing to catch our breaths and adjust our packs when, just a few feet to our left, there was a high-pitched, nerve-shattering scream. It sounded like a woman who was being torn limb from limb. We froze in our tracks and both of our flashlights shined immediately on Dad's face. He was amazingly calm, and carefully whispered, "Cougar. Get going." We double-timed it across the meadow.

Our hearts were pounding and shoulders aching as we turned the corner and saw the lights of the cabin and the smoke coming from the chimney. We all propped our freezing feet up close to the little stove, while Mom eagerly pored over the new books that would keep her company in the week ahead.

Nobody mentioned a word of our encounter to Mom, but you can believe it kept Dad, Doug, and me rattled for a good, long time.

###

A Sunday picnic with my Talbot grandparents.

In 1943, the year before our return to the cabin, Dad's parents had bought the remnants of a burned out farm. Nestled in a beautiful but isolated valley just over the hill from Pleasant Creek, "The Ranch" as we called it consisted of the remains of a homestead, barn, and some outbuildings. Beyond the homesite to the west were hayfields of perhaps twelve acres, framed by dense forest. Granddad built a garage/storage shed/tool shed, and then constructed a new house. It wasn't terribly big or fancy, but nonetheless a nicely built three-bedroom home. My grandparents kept a huge vegetable garden in the back. The setting in that little valley was idyllic.

A woman lived near the entrance to the road that split off from the county road and led to my grandparents' place. The road crossed her property, but they had an easement allowing access. In recent times, the land had been mined for gold, and a floating dredge sat in a nearby pond—a huge, floating, two-and-a-half-story structure about the size of a small Mississippi River sternwheeler. We learned it had come from Alaska. The dredge had devoured the land, passing it through the gold extraction process, then spitting out huge piles of bare rocks behind. Doug and I were given permission to fish in the dredge pond. There were some big fish in there, and we had some great times catching them.

The woman was reported to be the mistress of the guy who owned the dredge. She became good friends with my grandparents, playing bridge with them weekly and helping to enliven the sterile social scene.

Everything was fine until the woman apparently made a pass at Granddad. Her overtures were rebuffed, and it wasn't long before my grandparents learned that the road easement to their house had been revoked.

Somehow, Granddad was successful in purchasing land that would provide a new route to their home. We spent many weekends building the new half-mile driveway.

We never asked if our fishing permits were also revoked, but it seemed to go without saying.

One of my favorite things about my grandparents' place was their dog Shep, a beautiful collie. When we would visit the cabin in the years before moving there, we would always stop at

Mom with Shep.

my grandparents' before the last bit of the journey. As we'd leave for the cabin, Shep would run beside us for a remarkable distance. Remarkable not just for the sheer miles he put in, but because he was not running on the road, but paralleling us in the brush and trees flanking the road. Watching him keep up with us as he wove through the forest was a source of wonder to me. As the road would swing to the left, up some small little drainages, Shep would cut straight across the canyon and always meet us just as we came around the corner. This went on for some eight to ten miles, until we turned off the county road and started down the two ruts leading to the creek. We'd stop there, and Shep would plop down into the creek to cool off and drink. He was amazing.

When we moved to the cabin in the summer of '44, Shep came with us, to keep Mom company during the upcoming months when Doug and I would be away at school. After school started, he would often come down to the bus stop to meet us and walk us home.

One early winter day, Shep wasn't there to greet us when we got off the bus. We figured he'd gotten distracted by a squirrel along the way, but there was no sign of him on the hike home,

An inseparable threesome.

After we lost Shep, Boots joined the family to keep Mom company.

either. When we got to the cabin, the first thing we asked Mom was, "Is Shep here?" to which she answered, "You mean he wasn't there to meet you?" We couldn't believe something had happened to such a self-sufficient survivor, but after hours of calling his name and patrolling his usual haunts, there was no trace of him. We finally surmised he had probably slipped crossing the tree bridge across the creek, and fallen into the raging stream below.

Shep was soon replaced by a small brown puppy with white feet. Mom named him Boots. He kept her company during those long dark days of winter, when what little sunlight there was on our northeastern side of the mountain would be gone by early afternoon.

Money was very tight as Christmas 1944 approached. It was snowing and somewhat difficult to find the right tree, cut it down, and pull it back to the cabin. After getting it on a stand, it looked pretty naked compared to the trees we had become accustomed to. All of the traditional ornaments had been boxed and left in storage with our other household items back in Grants Pass. So, we made paper garlands, popcorn garlands, and even a few candles clamped to branches. The candles were lit only occasionally—they were expensive and we were often reminded of the fire danger and the stories of whole families lost in Christmas tree fires. The few ornaments were small pine cones painted or somehow colored.

Doug and I had been repeatedly warned to not expect too much in the way of gifts. As we looked under the tree, however, three long packages caught our eyes. The few gifts were handed around and within seconds, Doug and I were gazing upon two .22 single-shot rifles (one for each of us) and a single-shot 12-gauge shotgun (to be shared). Better still, there were boxes and boxes of ammunition! There could not have been two more happy boys in the world.

However, it was not such a happy day for the creatures of the forest—if it moved, we shot it, or more accurately, shot at it. Dad grilled us on hunter safety and soon turned us loose.

From then on, chores around the place got done with amazing speed and attention, for once they were all done, we could go hunting! I can well remember bagging my first big kill. I spotted a large grey squirrel and carefully stalked it. Spotting it sitting high in a tree, I carefully took aim and "crack"—to my amazement, the squirrel fell to my feet. I was amazed—I'd done it! And then I looked down at that beautiful animal, lying on his back with his furry white belly. His dead eyes seemed to look directly into mine, and I felt for the first time the ambivalence that would mark my brief time as a hunter. I would be lying if I said I didn't enjoy the sport and thrill of it. But that was my last squirrel. From then on, I only hunted game that would help put food on the table.

Chapter 9
Spring, 1934: Louise

Eventually *the long days of short days gave way to inklings of spring. The air was full of the scent of growing things. In my walks to the mailbox, my eyes were on the lookout for the first sproutings of wild flowers, or tree buds in the old orchard. The animals were in pairs; birds a-courting in the brush. I saw a pheasant one morning, wooing a rather drab female. It told a story just to watch them. He did every possible thing to attract her attention, and she deigned to notice him. The next time I passed that spot, I scared them out of the brush, with their family in full flight before them.*

By the time fresh green vegetables were in the markets, we were starved for them, but at their spring prices, couldn't possibly afford them. One morning Dougie and I took a knife and a couple of buckets, and set out to see what we could find in the way of wild greens. We picked and dug dandelions until the buckets were overflowing. Very proudly we carried them home, and I spent an hour or so cleaning them. Into a large pot they went to cook, using the lid to contain the bounty. What a disappointment when I lifted the lid to discover our harvest had been transformed to mere spoonfuls of dark, tightly packed greens. But, my oh my, did that mouthful tease our palettes!

Somewhere I had read that fiddleneck ferns in the early spring were very good to eat, and tasted something like asparagus. So, with curiosity, I gathered the fronds. They WERE just like asparagus, if a bit slick!

###

The Charlies had a cat, who had kittens, one of which I claimed. I named him Rasputin, for even as a tiny thing he was a devil. No one in those parts had ever heard of Rasputin the person and certainly had no idea how to pronounce the name. Another reason for them to think me queer: I named not only my cat, but all the chickens. The first hen I named Marie Antoinette, because although she was treated like royalty thanks to her productivity (one egg a day), her eventual fate was sealed. When I tried to explain why each and every creature was ticketed with a name, people got an odd look on their faces. So, I quit trying to tell them. Rasputin was the pet of the family, along with a bantam rooster who led a monastic life with us for a year before he had a mate. He was named Mister—and we addressed him with the respect that title denotes, for he was a direct son of a thoroughbred fighting cock someone had brought from Cuba. Mister was small but had spurs, and was clearly master of all he surveyed. The roosters who came to join our flock learned to respect him, even if he was only a third of their size.

As farfetched as it may sound, Mister and Rasputin were fast friends and playmates! Rasputin would get behind a small bush, and Mister, in all his gaily hued glory, would walk past as though he were entirely unaware of Rasputin. Out Rasputin would jump, in the manner of all kittens, and Mister would fly up into the air a couple of feet. Then, around the rooster would turn and, with his beak open and wings spread, chase Rasputin under the house. Time after time I watched them play out this scenario. When there was snow on the ground, they would chase and fight over the same descending flake.

Mister slept on the foot of Dougie's bed, and we needed no alarm clock, for with the break of day came his pesky crow—that is, once he finally learned to crow. His first efforts sounded like a boy of fourteen, with unexpected leaps into tenor from bass. I was close to hysterics listening to his "song" roller coaster up and down.

Finally, Rasputin grew into a regular tomcat, and we were afraid his instincts would get the better of him with regard to Mister. And so we obtained the hen I referred to earlier, to keep Mister contented. She was a banty, a darling little cream-colored thing, but with a wild streak.

When Mister made the hen's acquaintance, he wasn't at all interested in Rasputin, except to guard her from him because Rasputin, true to his breed, had turned his attention from Mister to the little hen. It took us almost a week to teach the rooster to go to spend the night with his mate in the henhouse instead of at the foot of Dougie's bed. He would escort her down to the henhouse at dusk, then come back up to the cabin, and hop up on the bed. We would take him back down to the henhouse, but, as if wondering if we silly people had taken leave of our senses, he would find a way out and back to the cabin. No sooner had we given up on trotting him down to the henhouse multiple times a night, than something apparently clicked in his tiny brain—and he decided to start joining his partner at night. Because of all the waiting Mister had put her through, I decided to call the little hen Patience. It was a sight to watch her teach Mister to scratch for bugs, and to venture farther away from the cabin each day. When she had chicks, she was motherhood embodied, with her doting, watchful care of them. As time went on, I eventually became the owner of quite a flock of chickens. I was as proud of those chickens as the normal city dweller is of his new Ford V-8. But, my joy in those chickens was short lived.

I had a letter from my mother saying she had read a new book that she knew I would enjoy: San Francisco—A Pageant, by Charles Caldwell Dobie. I immediately sent to the Oregon State Library for the book, then impatiently waited for sufficient time to pass for it to arrive at the mailbox. I was so thrilled to open the box and see that familiar wrapping. On the six-mile tramp home, I read three chapters while simultaneously negotiating a seven percent grade climb. I had always loved San Francisco, had read every book ever printed on the city, and never been quite satisfied with what I had read. This book was different—the best I had ever read at capturing all the magic of the city. Here were the words that perfectly described the top of Telegraph

Hill at sunset, the tinted adjectives that referred to Chinatown, the shadows of the old city in the days of the Peraltas and the Arguellos. That evening, Doug set out for the nearest town for several days, leaving me all alone with the children, my new book—and the chickens.

I cooked our evening meal, interspersed with snatches of the Mission Dolores, then washed the dishes, drying them with the book propped alongside the sink. I put the children to bed distracted by thoughts of Rezanov and his love for Concepcion, and finally got the boys to sleep muttering words about Mammy Pleasant and the earthquake. No book has ever laid such a spell upon me, outside of the old classics. I sat in the lamplight reading until 1 a.m., and when I had finally finished the book, it was with such a feeling of regret! I wanted that book to go on forever. I sat there alone—the fire had gone out, and suddenly I was cold—yet I could not go to sleep. I just had to share with someone how I felt about that book, and then I realized: Who better to tell than the author?

I found odds and ends of paper and, from the bottom of my homesick heart, poured out to Mr. C.C. Dobie my appreciation for his ability to capture San Francisco's charm in a book. After addressing the letter and stamping it (a sure guarantee that I would mail it, for I never had enough stamps), I finally went to bed.

Suddenly, Rasputin was jumping onto and off of the bed, wild with agitation. The moon had been full earlier, but now the night was black, with a hint of deep purple up above, where the fir and pine met the sky. Rasputin always woke me when there was anything about the house, so I suspected a porcupine outside. I started to tell him that if he expected to sleep with me, he would have to keep quiet or get off the bed when the air erupted with the sound of chickens squawking. I jumped out of bed in my nightgown (model 1928) and grabbed the flashlight. Out the door and over the porch railing I leaped. (I realized later what a hurdler I would have made—try taking a five-foot porch railing in the middle of the night!)

As I drew near the henhouse door, I proceeded slowly—something had forced the henhouse door open about six inches. Staring at the aperture, I listened. It was so still, standing in the inky darkness. I stiffened at the sound of feet—tiny feet, like those of a small terrier. It seemed an eternity that I held my breath, waiting.

Twice in my life I've had what I would guess is the feeling of abject fear, as though a scarf was being drawn tightly about my body—my lungs stifled, my heart doing loops up and down my throat. The first time I felt that flutter was when Doug and I applied for a marriage license. The second time was standing in that awful darkness, eyes glued to the henhouse door.

My hand shook as it held the flashlight. The batteries were on their last legs, and I strained my eyes at that crack until small dots of light danced before my eyes. Sure enough, the light first caught a brief movement, then eyes that glowed ruby red in the light: skunk! How on earth had it gotten through that tiny opening?

I ran to the cabin for the shotgun. My poor feet were bare, and the stones were sharp. Over the porch railing I vaulted, grabbed the gun, then hurdled back toward the chicken house. Two feet from the door, I stopped, trying to hold the flashlight along the barrel of the gun. Over to the left something moved! I swung the trembling gun and light—there were those two ruby ovals again. I fired. The flashlight dropped to the ground. Hands covered in perspiration, I reached for the light and the gun slid from my hands. After what was probably a few seconds but felt like hours, my clammy hands grasped the gun and the light. I clicked the breach, and realized that I'd fired my one and only shot.

Back to the cabin I flew, deafened by the shot. I grabbed a handful of shells and reloaded as I ran out the door. Halfway to the henhouse I stopped. A rustle in the brush to the right—my light tagged its body as it flashed by. Just as it burrowed under a fallen log, I fired. I thought afterward that if an orchestra had commenced, it would have played "Hearts and Flowers," for with the gracefulness of that slow-drifting melody, a certain scent—and not that of flowers—wafted into my nostrils.

It was all over. I knew that I could not open that chicken coop *door. I went back to the cabin, lit the lamp, and looked at the children. They had slept through the whole event. I threw on a bathrobe, put slippers on my sore feet, and ran to my nearest neighbors, the two Charlies. One came back to the cabin with me, built a fire, and suggested that he could do with a cup of hot chocolate (bless his heart, he knew I needed something to occupy my hands and mind). Then and only then did we go down to the hen house and open the door.*

There lay motionless all of my new pullets, and the little hen, Patience. The new baby chicks had disappeared altogether. Mister had not been touched! The first streaks of dawn created shadows next to the dead chickens. I felt as though I had lost a group of close friends—not to mention eggs for the coming months.

I had my letter to Mr. Dobie ready to mail, but couldn't resist opening and re-writing it to tell him what had happened after I'd stayed up so late reading his book. I mailed it the next day.

Every night while Doug was gone, I managed to have all of the wood and water in the house by nightfall. Nothing could persuade me to go out into the blackness that held such terror for me.

Doug returned a little more than a week later, bringing the accumulated mail. Amongst the letters, I saw one with a return address for a Mr. C.C. Dobie! My fingers became all fluttery, and I finally asked Doug to open the letter. My eyes first flew to the heading: East Bay Dramatic Society. Then, on to the contents: Mr. Dobie was sorry to have to decline their request of an appearance and lecture. I started laughing, explaining to Doug what had happened. I sat down that evening and wrote again to Mr. Dobie, enclosing the letter to the dramatic society and my suspicion that there had been a mix-up. Sure enough, several evenings later, Doug brought in the mail and with it, an autographed copy of Mr. Dobie's book and the letter I should have originally received. After our return to the Bay Area, I had the opportunity to meet Mr. Dobie and thank him for his kindness.

Chapter 10
Spring, 1945: Dave

In those mountains, winter was for making plans around all the stifled productivity that would be unleashed come spring, and for Dad those plans centered on the bridge to be built over Pleasant Creek. As soon as weather permitted, work on the project commenced. Building a span long enough to reach across Pleasant Creek and strong enough to support a car was no small undertaking.

Dad contracted with Abe Johnson to pull and station four big logs (called "stringers") across Pleasant Creek. I'm guessing the distance was perhaps forty feet.

Once the stringers were laid side-by-side and properly positioned, we chopped the bark and tried to smooth and even up the top surface as best we could. Then the real fun began. It was the job of Doug and me to head out and find the trees that would become log planking for cars to drive across, cut and limb those trees, then haul the logs to the bridge site.

We needed maybe seventy-five such logs. As a group, the trees had to be smallish and consistent in size; individually, they had to be uniform in trunk diameter—in other words, the trunk's size at the base of the tree had to be as close as possible to the trunk's size at the top. Anyone who knows how trees grow knows that trunk uniformity is not high on Mother Nature's list. I suspect my father knew what he was asking when he sent us on this mission, perhaps teaching us a lesson in perseverance. When we came upon one of these rare prizes, after some minor rejoicing, it would be cut, limbed, and hauled to the bridge site. Naturally, the more of these few-and-far-between trees we collected, the wider our search territory stretched, increasing the hauling time considerably. This phase of work alone took the better part of a day. When we were finished, we counted eighty logs, each about fourteen feet in length and maybe six inches across.

Next came the difficult and tedious job of peeling the logs. Conventional wisdom held that bugs would get into the bark and shorten the life of the log; peeling eliminated that risk. Debarking even one tree took more than an hour, and smaller trees were actually harder to peel than large ones. We were many days stripping the lot of them.

Finally, with the logs peeled and ready for their new assignment, we placed them across and perpendicular to the

(Left) Building the bridge across Pleasant Creek, spring 1945. Four huge stringer logs created the base. Then smaller logs that Doug and I had carefully chosen, cut, and peeled were secured on top. (Right) Atop the new bridge, Mom looks over our handiwork. In the winter, this serene little stream would become a raging torrent.

stringers and secured them with giant nails. I don't remember who was at the wheel for the maiden voyage over the bridge, but it was surely something for all of us to celebrate. Little did we know that while it wasn't a bridge to nowhere, its usefulness would be limited, as our move back to town would come abruptly in just a few short months.

There had been a small lean-to behind the cabin that at some point leaned too far and just fell over. The wooden shingles that were once its roof made excellent kindling—and they were conveniently located right outside the back door. This would have been an ideal situation for the fire builders and tenders, namely Doug and I, except for one pesky factor.

Rattlesnakes.

It seemed that besides excellent kindling, the old shakes also made an ideal home for rattlers. On more than one occasion the unmistakable buzz of rattles at the bottom of the pile let us know we had rudely interrupted a nap.

For some reason, that area of Southern Oregon was perfect rattlesnake habitat for two varieties—the smaller, feistier diamondbacks and the larger, less aggressive timber rattlers. Both had distinctive markings on their backs and triangular heads. Rattlesnakes hibernate in the winter in underground caves and caverns. So the time to be particularly watchful was late spring, summer, and fall. Rule Number One for Doug and me was to never run in the woods. Rule Number Two was to never jump over logs. Rule Number Three? Never put your hands where you can't see.

In the '20s and '30s, miners in the area had an ingenious method of holding down the snake population. They would somehow find the winter snake dens and throw sticks of dynamite into the caves. The miners had left long ago, though, and the snake population had more than fully recovered.

We soon learned that the best thing to do when you crossed paths with a snake was to freeze and hope it would peacefully continue on its way. If we showed respect and gave them space, they seemed to do likewise. While it was customary in those days to kill every rattlesnake you found, I can safely say that of all the encounters I had over the years, there was only one incident of the snake really wanting to fight. In all other cases, the snakes were doing everything possible to get away or hide.

Dad's rule of thumb regarding how close you could get to a rattlesnake was that it could strike about half the distance of its length. So, if it looked to be about five feet long, you wouldn't want to get closer than two and a half feet. When defending themselves, rattlers coil up in a series of tight "S" shapes. If provoked, they will attack by quickly uncoiling and literally launching themselves at you.

We soon learned to be especially careful in certain places: warm rocks bathed in sunlight; old rundown structures where mice, rats, and ground squirrels (their favorite meals) might be found; piles of wood shakes.

When you killed a rattlesnake, you made sure to cut off and bury its head, where the venom pockets were. The idea was that left out in the open, the snake would be consumed by yellow jackets (infamous meat-lovers), head and all. Then, when the yellow jacket stung you, its toxin would carry a bonus dose of snake venom. "You don't want to get stung by one of those babies," my father cautioned.

One spring day I was exploring at "the flats", the small open meadow that had once been home to the Charlies. There were lots of dilapidated outbuildings, a few apple trees, and the piles of pipe from their mining operations. I had been watching a digger squirrel near one of the pipe piles and got down on my hands and knees to see better. A small section of pipe obscured my view, and I gave it a little push. Sure enough, I was suddenly eye-to-beady-eye with a rattler. It's hard to say which of us was more surprised. I jumped back just as the snake struck. He missed. Fortunately for me, rattlesnakes have notoriously bad eyesight, relying on heat-sensing pits behind their nostrils to locate a target—not a highly accurate system. I'm fairly sure my heart did not resume beating until several minutes later.

Mom admires a timber rattler I had bagged. A more serious encounter between my mother and a rattlesnake would end our second stint at the cabin.

Chapter 11
Summer, 1934: Louise

By the time our second summer on the mountain came around, our supply of clothing—most of which we had arrived with—had almost given out. Not that there was much to be done about it. There was certainly no allowance for replacements. Before moving to the cabin, I had never done any mending. I knew a bit about darning, but only as part of an obligatory curriculum in school. Here, I had been confronted with sock holes of such proportions that the items were hardly recognizable. Dougie's overalls had worn ragged in the knees from his choo-choo trips around the cabin floor. Doug's jeans and shirts had been on the losing end of daily battles with the surrounding brush and briers.

My mother, always a fine seamstress, claimed that I handled a needle like a crowbar, and I am not in a position to argue. How I toiled—my hands shook and perspired until I could not pull the thread–weighted needle through even one thickness of cloth! My first pair of mended socks at the cabin looked like a small relief map of a French battlefield, complete with hummocks and trenches. I realized, after all the labor, that no one could possibly wear those bumpy things on their feet. The first few shirts were to laugh out loud at—in fact, my sense of humor was often the only thing that kept me from tears of frustration. But I persisted, and my skills improved. Still, by summer, it was good that the need for layers of sturdy clothes had diminished. Sturdy was not a word that could be used to describe much of anything around the cabin by then.

The women of the area had tried over the previous months to

start a sewing club. I was never able to attend one of these rare gatherings due to weather or a baby to care for, and by the time David was old enough to come along, the meetings had been discontinued due to lack of participation. From the descriptions given me, I judge that I missed some real occasions, though. The members of the circle always brought fancy work. After an hour or so of sewing, the hostess would retire to the kitchen and proceed to put a "bite" on the table. This "bite" was usually a lavish display of the hostess's culinary skill, although protocol required that she profusely apologize for the pittance that graced her board. There were certain recipes that enjoyed wide fame, such as Mrs. Hansen's blueberry cobbler, and Mrs. Becker's lightning cake. Recipes for everything from confections to home remedies were exchanged and discussed. It all sounded quite enjoyable, and I was sorry I never got to be part of the festivities.

We had been living at the cabin for almost a year before I came out for a trip to the big city—a visit to see my mother in San Francisco. I had always considered myself so cosmopolitan, but what I experienced on that excursion was nothing short of culture shock.

Throughout my childhood, I had heard of people "from the sticks." Lo and behold, I discovered to my surprise that I had become one of them! The traffic noises of the city were music to my ears, after the deafening silence of the hills. But crossing that traffic caused me more unrest than the long miles I had traveled to get there. I found myself full of twitters and jitters, and most unexpectedly homesick for the wilds of our mountain cabin. I discovered that boys and girls I had gone to school with were mostly married and raising families, like me. But that was where the similarities ended. I could not believe I had ever been friends with girls who thought the height of accomplishment was to throw a cocktail party for thirty or forty people, or to entertain some dignitary. Boys with whom I had gone out were joining the Rotarians and the Kiwanis, and their wives were so proud of them! It was not *my place to belittle these marks of social standing—but they seemed so far away and irrelevant, something quite foreign to myself, to my new ideas of what constituted life and its essentials.*

On the way home from my trip, when at last I came within calling distance of the cabin, my heart did loops. I covered the last fifty yards, straight up as it was, at a flat-out sprint.

But the heart of my home is a fickle one. Within six months, I found myself aching to get back to the city again. Away from the mind-numbing silences, and the monotony that mountain life invariably produced. As trite as it was, it seemed I was living proof of the old adage that wherever we are, we always long for greener pastures.

###

To the ordinary person of this modern day and age, radio is something taken for granted. Phonographs are practically passé, excepting for those few who want their music when and where they want it.

But it's hard to imagine just how hungry for music we were, and in the summer of 1934 we acquired a phonograph free of charge. What a phonograph it was: a vintage '14!

The phonograph came with six records, which we played over and over. To this day, I only have to hear the first few bars of those songs to immediately recognize them.

One summer day, we were in town getting supplies. As usual, we had no money to spend on anything but food—but as we drove along Main Street, I saw a music store closing out their stock. I knew in my bones that I would get in there somehow—and I did. There were Pisa-like towers of records everywhere, blanketed by years of dust. I went through each and every pile, eventually coming out with several treasures. Almost all were recordings of Leopold Stokowski conducting the Philadelphia Symphony Orchestra. It was a veritable gold mine—for only five cents apiece! Over the long summer evenings, those records were welcome company.

###

As our first anniversary of cabin living approached, I found myself reflecting on nothing short of a complete transformation in my life and sensibilities.

I had arrived with a sick six-week-old infant, worried about depriving him of the expert medical care he might need. That sick infant was now a thriving one-year-old who had known nothing but this home for the entirety of his short life. There had been times, though, when one or both of the children had been very sick, with the doctor many miles away over impassible roads. I had had to treat them myself, taking the risk of doing the wrong thing, then standing by and waiting to find out the verdict.

I had been achingly homesick for home and Mother, with her nice broad bosom to rest my head upon. Like steel is tempered through many tests, so had my character been made stronger.

Many of my San Francisco friends did not think we would last a year. Several of them even had bets as to just how long the Talbots would stay up in the mountains. When I would go home for a visit, everyone would say how very brave I was. Bravery had nothing to do it! I had no choice! I did not stay because I wanted to, but because I could not leave. I had no money of my own, and I loved my husband. There were times when I would have sold my soul to get out of those mountains, though! Times when I thought I would go stark raving mad from the monotony. Days when I took my tired nerves out on those I loved, and then felt ashamed. Bravery? No! I sometimes felt so sorry for myself that the tears would come and I could not stop them, feeling a fool for giving way to those feminine emotions. But I did learn what backbone and grit are, and what it means to go on in the face of physical and mental weakness.

Ultimately, the place and the people of those mountains had grown on me. At the end of our first year, I realized I was right where I wanted to be. I was raising my boys in a place where just living was a task, and where luxuries were few and far between, but so appreciated when received! Where there were only simple people, living simply. Where there was time for concentration, and contemplation.

I had been born and raised a city girl, but I had grown into a mountain woman.

Wilderness family, 1934.

Chapter 12
Summer, 1945: Dave

We had moved to the cabin a year earlier for a couple of reasons: one, to save money to pay off the huge hospital bill from Mom's miscarriage and cancer treatment. But there had also been talk about the mountain air helping with Mom's asthma and overall health. It was true that her asthma seemed better at the cabin. But as for her overall health, there was little evidence that the move had produced any real curative effects. In fact, she continued to have small "spells" that had started before the move; at any given time, her face might suddenly just go blank, as if her brain had been frozen for a few moments. If one of the episodes happened in the presence of Doug or me, we would say nothing and just look

On the front porch of the cabin, 1945.

at each other in a silent question. Neither we nor our parents ever spoke about it. It was also evident that the spirited spark that had always burned so brightly in her when we were younger seemed to have been doused. She didn't laugh or joke as much. As time went on, some days she just stayed in bed, surrounded by piles of her beloved books.

I'm sorry to say that in my self-centered world of pre-adolescence, my mother's health played a relatively small role. Her maladies were part of our routine; they were familiar, and so while a little disconcerting, also not particularly alarming.

Mom, Doug, and I had walked down to the creek to meet Dad on his way home from work. It was August 1945. Mom had her book and Doug and I had no trouble finding interesting things to do in the stream. As the time estimated for him to arrive came and passed, we became increasingly concerned. He was seldom late.

The sun left the creek bottom and we were about to begin the walk back to the cabin. Suddenly we all heard it: the distant mix of yelling voices and a car horn honking repeatedly. Confused and worried, we turned to the road as the cacophony drew closer.

As our car came into view, followed by another, we could see Dad's head out the window yelling at the top of his lungs, "VJ Day! VJ Day! Victory over Japan! The war's over! Japan has surrendered!"

I had never seen my father drunk before. Thankfully, two of his work buddies had brought him home. Mom drove us the rest of the way, with Dad belting out the news to the wilderness, "VJ Day! VJ Day!" Once home, Dad continued his revelry throughout the night, repeatedly wandering off into the woods. To find him, we just stood on the porch and yelled, "VJ Day!" From the darkness would come an impassioned echo, "VJ Day!" Then one of us would go off with a flashlight, find him, and bring him back to the cabin. He was not a pretty sight the next morning, but we all knew that his celebration had been more than just patriotic. For Dad, war's end meant that two brothers and a brother-in-law would be coming home safe.

Not long after that, Dad, Doug, and I were down working on the road. Doug happened to look up and yelled something. Dad and I raised our heads to see Mom staggering toward us. Her left leg was bandaged and seeping blood.

We ran toward her and as we got close, she blurted out, "Rattler."

Dad raced back up the hill to get the car while Doug and I tried to comfort Mom. Half-crying in fear and pain, she managed to explain what had happened. Going for a bucket of water, like we all had done hundreds of times, she had surprised a rattlesnake. It had struck instinctively, hitting her in the fleshy part of her left ankle, then slithered away, likely as frightened as she was.

We'd all been schooled on what to do in such a circumstance, and Mom had followed protocol. She'd gotten out the snakebite kit, taken the razor, and cut an "X" at each of the fang marks. Today snakebite treatment is much different, but back then, the idea was to quickly bleed out most of the venom before it got into the bloodstream. She then fashioned a crude tourniquet and started down the hill to find us.

Dad ruined four good tires getting her to the emergency room. She was one sick lady, and had to spend several days in the hospital, but recovered well. It came out later that an overeager doctor almost killed her with an overdose of antivenin.

###

We all knew the perils of our backwoods life, and had tried our best to steer clear of them. But caution and wilderness smarts can only take you so far. Sometimes danger just jumps out of nowhere and bites you—literally—and the consequences suddenly outweigh the advantages of living with risk. So it was that Dad decided it was time for us to move back to town.

While Mom was in the hospital and he was at work, it fell to Doug and me to get the cabin ready to close. Before Dad left for work one morning, he sat us both down.

"Boys, I hate to ask this of you, but you are going to have to kill your animals. I know this will be hard, but we can't waste the meat." His tone of voice seemed to assume we had formed some sort of loving bond with the livestock. No way. They had been nothing but work and a constant interruption to our free time. But Dad had left out one crucial part of the instruction: how to do it.

For two boys working on their hunting aim, this open-ended assignment clearly called for one methodology. Without a word between us, we grabbed our .22s and ammunition. We'd take turns running down to the chicken coop and rabbit hutches, letting out three or four animals at a time. They'd race off in all directions, and we turned it into a big-game hunt. I had no ambivalence over this assignment—as Dad had said, we needed the food.

When the hunt was over, we skinned and plucked and gutted and wrapped what would become many fall and winter dinners. No one ever questioned the holes that riddled the meat on our plates.

###

We moved back to Grants Pass and life went on. Dad had a shorter commute to work. Mom recovered from the snakebite, but still preferred her bed and books on many days. Doug was able to focus on basketball and girls. I soon fell in with the advantages of being a townie, reacquainting myself with old friends and favorite haunts.

I missed the cabin and our lives there, though, underestimating the potency of unbridled freedom and the sense of dominion over everything around me. Instead of an attachment to the chickens and rabbits, I had forged bonds with the trees, the creeks, the terrain, and my mind smoothed the hard edges of subsistence there to create a memory as constant and warm as the fires we dutifully tended.

POSTSCRIPT

In the years after we moved back to town, Mom's health continued to decline. She finally succumbed to a massive cerebral hemorrhage in 1960 at age fifty, fifteen years after our second (and last) stay at the cabin. Her "spells" continued in the years preceding her death, and I suspect they were not unrelated to the hemorrhage.

When Mom died, I was married and living in Grants Pass as well, with my wife Ann and our two small children, Eric and Sara. I was serving as Director of the City Parks and Recreation Department.

Soon after, Dad moved to San Diego where Doug and his wife and children lived. Dad married again and had a wonderful life until he died of colon cancer in 1982 at the age of seventy-three.

When Dad's father died in 1961, the cabin and the 640 acres where it stood were sold as part of the estate. None of us ever returned.

Over time, the lessons of that year in the mountains have changed for me, some becoming clearer, others less so.

Despite her earlier self-assessments as an out-of-place city girl, what a resourceful, resilient person my mother turned out to be—keeping four people fed, washed, clothed, and nurtured, under the most primitive conditions, over two lengthy stays.

I marvel at my dad, up at 5 a.m. every morning in order to drive the twenty-seven miles out and be at work in Grants Pass by

7 a.m. How did he know how to build that bedroom addition to the cabin? How did he have the courage to expect my brother and me to act as men at the ages of eleven and thirteen?

Brother Doug teases me now that I was a lazy, no good, whining slacker that he had to constantly prod into doing any work at all. I know better, and also know that we've never been closer than we were that year—a shared experience that runs deep in our blood.

As for me, I hope to never again have to fell, cut, limb, peel, or carry a log. Or, take care of chickens. Or, shoot a squirrel. Or, regularly carry books, canned goods, or anything, really, on my back, over miles of knee-deep snow. I learned that I could do a lot of things and was about as capable as I needed to be—both good stringers on which to build the framework of self-confidence. Thanks to Doug's "encouragement," I discovered work was not a four-letter word, but an essential ingredient in virtually all types of success. Along those lines, I also learned the fruitlessness of excuses; in fact, many years later, as I was trying to explain how much better I was going to run "next time" to University of Oregon Track Coach Bill Bowerman, he stopped me, looked me in the eyes, and simply said, "Hey Talbot—just do it." A prophetic directive from the grandfather of one of the world's most celebrated enterprises.

Mostly, through the rich web of interdependence we guilelessly wove, I learned the unflagging value of family, in the places they call home. I am there often in my head, pulling a small trout out of Three Pools, playing three-handed bridge with Mom and Doug, and popping ticks on the red-hot stovetop.